UNLOCKING THE

REALMS OF

BLESSING

FAVOR &

INCREASE

POSITIONED FOR PROSPERITY

Unlocking The Realms Of Blessing, Favor & Increase

THANK YOUS

I want to thank all the spiritual mentors who have poured into my life a revelation of generosity. It's this revelation that has propelled our ministry into the four corners of the earth, and has always enabled us to be positioned for prosperity. During the early years of my ministry, much of my understanding was shaped through the Word of God by the godly influence and mentorship of Pastor Bill C. Wilson and Pastor D. Karl Thomas. I am forever grateful for the impact and anointing they both imparted into my life. Also, a special thanks to my dear friend, Pam Couch for encouraging me to write this book and the revelations that God has personally given to me in regards to supernatural finances. As always, many thanks to the team that helped bring this book together: Melanie Hart, David Sluka, Ken Vail, and Janet Angela Mills.

Books by Joshua Mills

31 Days To A Miracle Mindset

31 Days Of Health, Wealth & Happiness

Advanced School Of Miracles

Atmosphere

Into His Presence – Praise & Worship Manual

Ministry Resources 101

Personal Ministry Prayer Manual

Positioned For Prosperity

School Of Miracles, Volume I

School Of Signs & Wonders, Course I

School Of Signs & Wonders, Course II

Simple Supernatural

Simple Supernatural Study Guide

Third Day Prayers

Time & Eternity

Available online 24/7 at:

www.NewWineInternational.org

TABLE OF CONTENTS

FOREWORD
BY REV. DON STEWART

God has given us all things that pertain to life and Godliness (2 Peter 1:3). This includes riches and wealth in the kingdom of God. There are different schools of thought in the Church today concerning poverty and prosperity. I believe it's very important to look at God's Word on these matters to understand that the true purpose of prosperity is to expand God's work and the kingdom of heaven throughout the entire world, For Jesus said, *"And this gospel of the kingdom will be preached in the whole world as a testimony to all nations..."* (Matthew 24:14).

When I was given the opportunity to write the foreword for this tremendous book, *Positioned For Prosperity,* by my good friend Joshua Mills, it felt as if my heart skipped a beat. It was almost as if I was carried back to the late 1950s as I would sit at the feet of my mentor Rev. A.A. Allen as He taught God's revelation about prosperity, which was all very new and foreign to many in the Body of Christ in those days. How thrilled I am as I read the anointed words of this book, *Positioned For Prosperity,* to know that this revelation and the truths taught to me as a young man are now being passed on to this generation.

In this book, Joshua will teach you how to love people and use money. The world (and sadly the Church) has had it backwards. Often they use people and love money. His practical no-nonsense approach is so refreshing that the Word is going to come alive to you as you read. You will begin to understand that God has unlimited prosperity for you in His kingdom if you are positioned to receive it.

I know of no one better qualified to help you receive a financial breakthrough in your life than Joshua Mills!

Follow the Biblical instructions that Joshua gives you in this book and I know that you will receive the financial breakthroughs you have longed for. These God-inspired words are Spirit and life. Obey these miracle instructions for they are life and will cause you to be **Positioned For Prosperity**!

Rev. Don Stewart
President, The Don Stewart Association
Founder of Feed My People
Phoenix, Arizona

*There is a blessing
on the other side of every tithe.*

*There is financial favor
on the other side of every offering.*

*There is an intended harvest
on the other side of every seed.*

*The key is that
they must all be released
into the glory
in order for you to experience
the miracle at the other side!*

~Joshua S. Mills

CHAPTER ONE

$\mathcal{G}$OING TO THE NEXT LEVEL

I have learned to be content whatever the circumstances.
I know what it is to be in need, and I know what it is to
have plenty. I have learned the secret of being content in any
and every situation, whether well fed or hungry, whether
living in plenty or in want. <u>I can do everything through
him who gives me strength</u>. ~Philippians 4:11-13

At the beginning of our marriage, Janet Angela and I lived in a little apartment with "blow-up" furniture. We didn't have enough money to buy a real couch, so we purchased an inflatable one! We also slept on a camping air mattress and endured many sleepless nights as the mattress would suddenly pop after too many months of use. During these times we didn't have the money to be able to buy quality furniture, nice clothes, or eat out at fine restaurants… let alone purchase airline tickets to travel to the nations! We learned how to live by simple means as we did the work of the ministry in our local church, and held several part-time jobs on the side. Hard work is one key to success that can never be underestimated!

*Y*ou will never complain about the place where God has called you to be if you realize that it is always the place of blessing. ~Joshua Mills

Maybe you are at this same point in your life right now. You've been working very hard and seeing very little profit from your efforts. There is a light at the end of this tunnel!

If you don't have a job that is paying you money – that is your problem. Stop reading this book and go get a job! God will never tell you to quit your job and begin living off of somebody else's hard-earned money! In His Word God says that He will bless the works of *your* hands!

"*Lazy hands make a man poor, but diligent hands bring wealth.*" (Proverbs 10:4)

Once you get a job, pick this book back up and you will find it very useful in revealing truths to your spirit that will put you in a place to be **Positioned For Prosperity**. Do you part and God will do His part.

These revelations that I am going to unfold throughout this book all started as seeds in my spirit back during our days of lack. It was through my obedience to these revelations that have caused us to prosper and be able to minister in the capacity that God has called us. Every *revelation* demands an *activation* in order to produce a *manifestation*!

Within the Scriptures the Apostle Paul shared that he had learned how to be content no matter the situation. I can also say that in my life I have learned how to be thankful in times of poverty and also in times of great prosperity. I am thankful for God's faithfulness and His willingness to bless His children as we reach out in faith to receive what He has already provided by grace.

Even though I've learned how to be thankful in times of lack, I will tell you that the times of prosperity are much better! Don't let anybody ever tell you that money will ruin your life. If you have the right attitude about it, it won't! It will simply enhance whatever is already happening in your life.

We make a living by what we get; we make a life by what we give. ~Winston Churchill, British Wartime Prime Minister

As the Lord has allowed Janet Angela and I to be responsible over greater finances in our ministry, it has simply enhanced our outreach and the ability to do what He has called us to do! It's impossible to fulfill your vision without a means of provision. It's impossible to do the work of the ministry unless you have financial resources!

- With money we have gone on costly missionary journeys to India, China, Japan, Indonesia, Brazil, Mexico, Haiti and many other foreign nations.
- With money we have sent thousands of Bibles across the Canadian Arctic and around the world.
- With money we have sponsored children in third world nations, taken care of the widows, and fed the poor.

- With money we have hosted spiritual training seminars and conferences around the world that required great faith for finances.
- With money we have manufactured and given away multiple thousands of books, CDs, DVDs and other life-changing resources.

It has taken money to do these things! I can say that the Lord has blessed me with finances to be able to do those things, and I am truly thankful for it. Both in my times of lack and in my times of prosperity I have learned how to be grateful for all things and how to praise the Lord in all situations. I can tell you though, walking in prosperity is a whole lot better than being in poverty. I am not bragging about it, I just want to make a point. It's hard to do the things that God has called you to do without the financial ability to support the vision.

Real generosity doesn't care if it's tax deductible or not! ~Anonymous

> *For the love of money is a root of all kinds of evil. Some people, eager for money, have wandered from the faith and pierced themselves with many griefs.* (1 Timothy 6:10)

Sometimes people argue using the statement that "money is evil" or that "money changes people." First of all, money is not evil. It is a useful tool that God wants us to manage properly in order to fulfill His call on our lives. However, if we begin to love money (or as some translations say begin "craving money") that is an evil thing to do, and we need to keep our hearts right about finances so that we don't fall into that trap.

But even more importantly, I want to tell you that money NEVER changes people. In my life money has never changed who I am, but as I have been blessed financially, it has allowed me to be MORE of who I am! Do you understand what I'm saying? I have been able to minister more effectively as an increase of finances have flowed into our ministry because it has enabled me to do what God has put on my heart to do.

> *In order to receive a gift from God you must first believe that He wants you to have it! ~Joshua Mills*

Several years ago a pastor invited me to come and minister at his church in the Northwest. It was a small church and they didn't have very much money, so the pastor told me that they were unable to pay for my airplane ticket.

I asked the Lord if I should go on this ministry trip because I didn't have the finances to cover the flight, but after prayer I felt as though I should go. At the time I didn't have the faith to believe for an airplane ticket, but when I found out that a seat on the bus would only cost me $49 round-trip, I had the faith to believe for that! I asked the Lord for the money to pay for the bus ticket and sure enough I got the money! Pinpoint your goals and be determined in your believing because the Lord always responds to faith.

I was so excited to go on this trip! It took me three days to get from London, Canada, to Seattle, Washington, but the whole time I was just praising the Lord! I was so thankful that I had the ability to get to where I knew I needed to be! There is always a way for you to be a blessing! Don't ever think you don't have enough. You may not have an airplane ticket... but if the Lord gives you a busfare... you just praise the Lord for it! When I got off the bus, my clothes were dirty and I probably smelled a little bit. I remember getting to the pastor's house and getting into the shower right away. When I took my shirt off, I could see a grey line all around my neck where my skin had been exposed to the seat. I was really dirty! I had never been so thankful for a shower in my entire life!

I was once young and now I am old, but not once have I been witness to God's failure to supply my need when first I had given for the further- ance of His work. He has never failed in His promise, so I cannot fail in my service to Him. ~William Carey, Missionary to India

While I was washing off, the Lord gave me a new song and I will never forget it! I was so thankful to be in the place that God had called me to be. You will never complain about the place where God has called you to be if you realize that it is always the place of blessing.

Two days later as I was preaching in the church, there was an airline pilot in those meetings. He received a fresh touch from the Lord, and at the end of the meeting he approached me about my trip to Seattle. He asked what airline I had flown because he wanted to offer me a first-class upgrade if I had flown with American Airlines. I proceeded to tell the pilot that I had taken the greyhound bus all the way from the other side of the continent. Immediately he stopped me and said, "I have many airline points and I would like to bless you with a first-class airline ticket." I told him once again that I hadn't flown on the airline, so I wouldn't be able to upgrade to a better fare. He clarified for me, "I would like to give you a first-class airline ticket. I want to bless you and give you a ticket for the rest of your ministry trip!"

Praise the Lord! God took my obedience in purchasing a bus ticket and changed it into a first-class airfare! If Jesus Christ could change the water into wine, why don't you think He can change your situation and turn things around for you? Remember this:

In order to be upgraded to first class, you must be willing to let go of your economy.

I have been able to travel around the world and minister in almost forty nations over the past nine years because I have had the finances to do so! These finances have always come by faith. In the natural I have never had a guarantee that I will be able to make it to the next month.

Generosity begins at home and generally dies from a lack of outdoor exercise."
~Anonymous

But by faith we have lived month to month, year to year, able to be a blessing to the nations! I believe being faithful with the little bus ticket has allowed us to experience the greater glory! Let me tell you, it has been a walk of faith and one money miracle after another, but God watches over His Word to perform it.

If you're faithful to be obedient, there is an unstoppable blessing that will come into your life also. God wants to take you to new levels of provision, but you must be willing to go to the next level! You must be willing to be stretched! You must be faithful with the little so that God can greatly expand your capacity to receive! You must be willing to go to the next level of generosity! You must be willing to allow God to change your thinking about money. Selwyn Hughes, an English pastor and author, said, *"**Remember this – you can't serve God and money, but you can serve God with money**."*

FIVE IMPORTANT FACTS ABOUT MONEY

1. MONEY IS AN IMPORTANT TOOL

Money is an important tool that God wants to allow to flow *to* us so that it can flow *through* us! This tool will enable you to do the things that God has called you to do. Money is a tool that should magnify the purposes of God in your life. *"**The rich rules over the poor and the borrower becomes the lenders slave**."* (Proverbs 22:7)

2. MONEY MAGNIFIES WHATEVER IS IN YOUR HEART

The Bible tells us that there is a correlation between the location of our money and the true attitude of our heart. You will only invest in whatever you believe in! *"For where your treasure is, there your heart will be also."* (Matthew 6:21)

3. MONEY SHOULD ALWAYS BE USED TO SERVE GOD

The foolish serve themselves with money; the wise serve God with money and realize that He is their source of true prosperity. Financial investments into the glory realm are the only ones that are guaranteed to never fail. *"No one can serve two masters. Either he will hate the one and love the other, or he will be devoted to the one and despise the other. You cannot serve both God and Money."* (Matthew 6:24)

> *Revelation demands an activation in order to produce a manifestation!*
> ~Joshua Mills

4. MONEY IS A TOOL FOR GLOBAL HARVEST

God is able to reap a greater harvest in the earth as you financially invest in the salvation of souls, the miracle of healing, and the advancement of the good news of the Gospel. *"...Not one church shared with me in the matter of giving and receiving, except you only; for even when I was in Thessalonica, you sent me aid again and again when I was in need. Not that I am looking for a gift, but I am looking for what may be credited to your account."* (Philippians 4:15-17)

5. MONEY ALWAYS EXPOSES A POVERTY SPIRIT

Wherever there is a resistance to receiving money, talking about money or using money, a poverty spirit is in operation attempting to keep the people of God bound in chains of lack. The Bible is clear that God is the one who gives us the ability to become prosperous! *"But remember the Lord your God, for it is he who gives you the ability to produce wealth, and so confirms his covenant, which he swore to your forefathers, as it is today."* (Deuteronomy 8:18)

What hinders most Christians is rarely something complicated. Everybody is always looking for an elaborate revelation. I've discovered that the Gospel truths of God's Word are actually quite simple. I even wrote an entire book called *Simple Supernatural* that deals with the basics of living in the glory realm. Often we don't have major problems in finances that need to be overcome, but rather minor adjustments in our revelation about generosity that need to be made. God's Spirit is generous, and when you begin to receive His mind about the situation, you will no longer find yourself struggling with lack, but suddenly set free by the limitless supply available in the glory realm.

The Bible says, *"My people are destroyed for lack of knowledge"* (Hosea 4:6). There is a poverty spirit in the Church that has been trying to withhold the knowledge of the Glory. There is a "knowledge of the Glory of the Lord" that will fill the earth just like the waters cover the sea. But there has also been a poverty spirit that has tried to withhold that knowledge of the true revelation of God's Spirit and His Word. This poverty spirit that comes from the

It is possible to give without loving, but it is impossible to love without giving.
~Amy Carmichael, Missionary to India

enemy tries to hold back the revelation because then the people can't enter into the Truth.

Now the Bible says that you shall know the Truth and this knowledge of the Truth is what will set you free (see John 8:32). Are you ready to be set free? Why don't you declare this right now! Just say it out loud, "I'm going to be set free." Go grab your wallet or purse right now and decree over your finances, "I'm going to be set free IN my finances in Jesus' name!"

Jesus Christ is the Spirit of Truth and if you've given your life to Him, He's alive inside of you! (If you haven't given your life to Christ yet, turn to the beginning of chapter 8 and pray to receive Christ). The Bible says that the Spirit of truth will lead you into all truth

> *There is nothing in life that you need that God has not already desired for you to have.*
> *~Joshua Mills*

(see John 16:13), and that's exactly what God is going to do for you through this book: Lead you into a greater revelation of the truth.

One of the ways that His truth is being revealed is through the Word of God. In this book I'm going to take you step by step through the glorious pages of the Gospel so that you will see how God desires to prosper your life. This is not a materialistic message, but one of absolute importance in order for the kingdom of God to advance in the earth. God wants to take you to the next level! I'm going to lead you into the realms of blessing, favor and increase – and I will even show you how to live and walk in these realms for the rest of your life!

This truth is about to touch your spirit with revelation that will set you free in every circumstance you will face in the days ahead. Are you ready to go deeper into these revelations of prosperity? Are you ready to go to the next level? Are you ready to receive something new from the Lord? *YES SIR* :)

Don't put your seat belt on. You'd better take it off right now because the Holy Spirit desires to launch you into the outer limits of the glory realm!

Get ready… get set… here we go!!!

OK :)

CHAPTER TWO

$\mathscr{F}$INANCIAL BREAKTHROUGH

One who breaks open the way will go up before them; they will break through the gate and go out. Their king will pass through before them, the Lord at their head. ~Micah 2:13

God is a God of breakthrough and He wants you to experience a financial breakthrough. The Bible says that God has already gone up before you and broken through for you! Before it began it was already finished. Christ declared it at Calvary (John 19:30). Before you ever got your problems, you had been given a breakthrough. The problem isn't the reality of your situation; the biggest problem is your perception of it.

Money isn't evil and finances are not supposed to be a problem for you. God owns a cattle on a thousand hills (Psalm 50:10); the earth is the Lord's and the fullness thereof (Psalm 24:1); the heavenly kingdom is filled with treasures and riches (Philippians 4:19). Everything you will ever need in life has already been provided for you through the shed blood of Jesus

Christ on the cross of Calvary. The question is what are you going to do about it? How will you respond to the gift of God? Are you ready to obtain your breakthrough?

Your salvation was obtained through the blood (Romans 5:9; Ephesians 1:7). Your healing was provided for through the blood (1 Peter 2:24). And your breakthrough into an over-coming life of hope and prosperity was already taken care of through the blood (Revelation 12:11). But each one of these blessings requires faith to receive what has been provided through grace. Every breakthrough has already taken place in the realm of the Spirit. Now you need to lay hold of it in the natural. The most powerful weapon of your warfare is the power of your choice!

Stewardship is the act of organizing your life so that God can spend you.
~Lynn A. Miller, Author

All throughout the Scriptures we can find divine radicals who pursued the purposes of God for supernatural breakthrough:

- Following the specific commands of the Lord, Joshua received a breakthrough as the walls of Jericho came tumbling down. (Joshua 6:1-5)
- God used Queen Esther to break through for the Jewish people because of her choice to become forceful in her faith! (Esther 4:13-14)
- Peter listened to the instructions of a "Breakthrough Angel" and escaped the cruel confinements of the prison cell and the horror of a public death trial. (Acts 12:6-11)

"From the days of John the Baptist until now, the kingdom of heaven has been forcefully advancing, and forceful men lay hold of it." (Matthew 11:12)

Do you want a breakthrough? You've got to become "forceful" in your faith! You must really know that you know that God desires to do something for you, and when you know it's from the Lord, you must purpose in your heart that you WILL receive it... no matter what the natural circumstance has predicted.

I have researched the Scriptures and found nine powerful reasons why God wants you to experience a financial breakthrough! As you read these, allow them to go deep into your spirit and begin to forcefully lay hold of these truths. This revelation will give you an impartation that will produce a manifestation!

I shovel money out, and God shovels it back... but God has a bigger shovel!
~R.G. LeTourneau, American Inventor

9 REASONS WHY GOD WANTS YOU TO EXPERIENCE A FINANCIAL BREAKTHROUGH!

1. YOU NEED MORE MONEY

It doesn't matter whether you're the poorest of the poor or the richest of the rich, you need more money to accomplish what God desires to place inside your heart. It requires provision to fulfill a vision, and it takes money to make dreams come true! *"A feast is made for laughter, and wine makes life merry, but money is the answer for everything."* (Ecclesiastes 10:19)

2. YOU NEED TO TAKE GOOD CARE OF YOUR FAMILY

God doesn't want your children to wear old tattered clothing or miss out on a good education. You need a financial breakthrough in your life so that you can take good care of your family's financial needs. Every parent is responsible to make sure that their children have been provided for financially and given what they need to accomplish their God given dreams! *"If anyone does not provide for his relatives, and especially for his immediate family, he has denied the faith and is worse than an unbeliever."* (1 Timothy 5:8)

3. YOU NEED TO LEAVE AN INHERITANCE FOR YOUR CHILDREN

Not only does God desire for you to leave a godly heritage and spiritual inheritance for your children, but God wants you to also leave a financial inheritance as a physical sign of God's blessing on your family lineage. The Bible says that a "good man" will do this! *"A good man leaves an inheritance for his children's children, but a sinner's wealth is stored up for the righteous."* (Proverbs 13:22)

4. YOU NEED TO PAY YOUR BILLS, TAXES, AND FINANCIAL OBLIGATIONS

I have seen too many Christians slacking on their bills and financial obligations. Throughout the years I have even witnessed other ministries on the brink of bankruptcy because they have not understood that God desired to give them a financial breakthrough! God's ability far exceeds our natural stupidity! In other words, when you've messed up and made bad business decisions, there is still a miracle for you. God wants you to be a person of your word – not forsaking your debt for others to pay.

"But so that we may not offend them, go to the lake and throw out your line. Take the first fish you catch; open its mouth and you will find a four-drachma coin. Take it and give it to them for my tax and yours." (Matthew 17:27)

5. YOU NEED TO INVEST IN MISSIONS AND SENDING THE GOSPEL AROUND THE WORLD

Not only does God want to give you enough money to take care of your current needs and the needs of your immediate family, but God wants you to invest into the spiritual well-being of the nations! How will the Gospel message be heard unless somebody preaches? How will the missionaries be able to go unless somebody sends them? *"And now, brothers, we want you to know about the grace that God has given the Macedonian churches. Out of the most severe trial, their overflowing joy and their extreme poverty welled up in rich generosity. For I testify that they gave as much as they were able, and even beyond their ability. Entirely on their own, they urgently pleaded with us for the privilege of sharing in this service to the saints. And they did not do as we expected, but they gave*

> *It takes money to make money! Give and it will be given back to you!*
> *~Joshua Mills*

themselves first to the Lord and then to us in keeping with God's will. So we urged Titus, since he had earlier made a beginning, to bring also to completion this act of grace on your part. But just as you excel in everything—in faith, in speech, in knowledge, in complete earnestness and in your love for us—see that you also excel in this grace of giving." (2 Corinthians 8:1-5)

6. YOU SHOULD GIVE TO THE POOR AND NEEDY

When you become generous in giving to the poor, the Bible says that you are lending to the Lord. Giving to the poor is truly a sign of generosity because in the natural they cannot repay you – but God will reward you for your efforts. *"He who is kind to the poor lends to the Lord, and he will reward him for what he has done."* (Proverbs 19:17)

7. YOU NEED TO INVEST IN YOUR SPIRITUAL LEADERS

This includes financially investing into the lives of your Pastors, Teachers, Evangelists and others who provide you with spiritual food. The Bible sets forth the principle of sowing and reaping. If you desire to walk in a specific anointing of the Holy Spirit, you must invest your finances into it! My friend Dr. Mike Murdock has said, "Whatever you make happen for others, God will make happen for you!" Do not withhold your finances from spiritual leaders, but see them as a God-given opportunity to partake of the same blessing that resides in their lives. *"The elders who direct the affairs of the church well are worthy of double honor, especially those whose work is preaching and teaching. For the Scripture says, 'Do not muzzle the ox while it is treading out the grain,'and 'The worker deserves his wages.'"* (1 Timothy 5:17-18)

8. YOU NEED TO INVEST IN KINGDOM CONNECTIONS

God wants to give you a financial breakthrough so that you can be the most generous person ever! He wants you to experience the supernatural doors of favor that open up as you bring your financial gift! It will cause you to access the door to divine appointments and bring you before kings, queens and great leaders. *"A gift opens the way for the giver and ushers him into the presence of the great."* (Proverbs 18:16)

> *Giving is more than a responsibility – it is a privilege; more than an act of obedience – it is evidence of our faith.*
> *~William Arthur Ward, American Educator*

9. GOD TAKES DELIGHT IN YOUR PROSPERITY!

Poverty is a curse from the enemy that cripples a person's ability to do what God has called them to do. Poverty causes sickness, disease, malnutrition, lack of education and ultimately results in death. At the start of the 21st century, the world's second biggest killer of children was unclean water in areas of poverty.[1] I hate the spirit of poverty – it is a killer of God's dreams and visions. The Lord desires for all of His children to walk in divine provision and supernatural prosperity! *"Let them shout for joy and rejoice, who favor my vindication; And let them say continually, "The Lord be magnified, Who delights in the prosperity of His servant."* (Psalm 35:27)

Freedom is coming to you as the Lord catapults you into the revelation found within the pages of this book. You're going into the three realms of blessing, favor and increase! That's a three cord strand that's not going to be broken. Hallelujah! I want you to say, "I'm not going to stay broke." Maybe you need to yell that and look that poverty spirit in the face and say, "I'm not going to stay broke! I don't care what's happened in the past; I don't care what it looked like before. But from this day on, I am not going to stay broke!" Hallelujah!

In all my years of service to the Lord, I have discovered a truth that has never failed and has never been compromised. That truth is that it is beyond the realm of possibilities that one has the ability to out give God. Even if I give the whole of my worth to Him, He will find a way to give back to me much more than I gave."
~Charles Spurgeon, English Baptist Pastor

"When they had all had enough to eat, he said to his disciples, "Gather the pieces that are left over. Let nothing be wasted." So they gathered them and filled twelve baskets with the pieces of the five barley loaves left over by those who had eaten." (John 6:12-13)

The Bible says that when Jesus blessed and broke the loaves, the bread and fish began to multiply with such abundance that provision not only came to the thousands gathered in that place, but there was an OVERFLOW of provision – so much so that twelve basketfuls were left over (see Matthew 14:13-21). In the area of finances, you may not have had enough for today, let alone leftovers for tomorrow. This is not the way it should be. Instead of being moved by our circumstances, we need to be moved by God's covenant of blessing.

One of the amazing names of God is El Shaddai. This name means "the God of more than enough!" Declare right now, "I am breaking through the brokenness and coming into a new dimension of multiplication!" You're on your way from "broke" to "breakthrough!" You're on your way from "not enough" to "more than enough!" Praise God!

CHAPTER THREE

THE THREE REALMS OF GENEROSITY

Though one may be overpowered, two can defend themselves. A cord of three strands is not quickly broken. ~*Ecclesiastes 4:12*

Did you know that the words *give, giving* and *gave* are mentioned over 4,000 times in the King James Version of the Holy Bible? God has a lot to say to us through His Word about financial matters. All throughout Scripture we are encouraged to be generous in everything we do! Here are some amazing truths about generosity.

20 IMPORTANT TRUTHS ABOUT GENEROSITY

1. GOD'S SPIRIT IS THE SPIRIT OF GENEROSITY

"If any of you lacks wisdom, he should ask God, who gives generously to all without finding fault, and it will be given to him." (James 1:5)

2. GENEROSITY IS ALWAYS A CHOICE

> *"Out of the most severe trial, their overflowing joy and their extreme poverty welled up in rich generosity."* (2 Corinthians 8:2)

3. WE ARE COMMANDED THROUGH GOD'S WORD TO SHOW GENEROSITY

> *"Command them to do good, to be rich in good deeds, and to be generous and willing to share."* (1 Timothy 6:18)

4. AS WE BECOME GENEROUS WITH OTHERS, WE WILL RECEIVE GENEROSITY OURSELVES

> *"A generous man will himself be blessed, for he shares his food with the poor."* (Proverbs 22:9)

5. YOUR GENEROSITY PRODUCES PRAISE TOWARDS GOD

> *"You will be made rich in every way so that you can be generous on every occasion, and through us your generosity will result in thanksgiving to God."* (2 Corinthians 9:11)

6. GENEROSITY ALWAYS PRODUCES PROSPERITY

> *"A generous man will prosper; he who refreshes others will himself be refreshed."* (Proverbs 11:25)

7. **GENEROSITY RELEASES A BLESSING FOR YOUR FAMILY LINEAGE**

"They are always generous and lend freely; their children will be blessed." (Psalm 37:26)

8. **GOOD OPPORTUNITIES WILL COME TO THOSE WHO WALK IN INTEGRITY THROUGH THEIR GENEROSITY**

"Good will come to him who is generous and lends freely, who conducts his affairs with justice." (Psalm 112:5)

9. **GENEROSITY OPENS THE DOOR FOR KINGDOM CONNECTIONS**

"Many curry favor with a ruler, and everyone is the friend of a man who gives gifts." (Proverbs 19:6)

10. **GENEROSITY IS AN OUTWARD SIGN OF AN INWARD CONVERSION**

"The wicked borrow and do not repay, but the righteous give generously." (Psalm 37:21)

11. **FINANCIAL SACRIFICE IS A SPIRITUAL INDICATOR OF A GENEROUS HEART**

"Take a sacred offering for the Lord. Let those with generous hearts present the following gifts to the Lord: gold, silver, and bronze." (Exodus 35:5 NLT)

12. GENEROSITY SHOULD BECOME A WAY OF LIFE

"But generous people plan to do what is generous, and they stand firm in their generosity." (Isaiah 32:8)

13. GENEROSITY RELEASES THE FRAGRANCE OF HEAVEN INTO ANY SITUATION

"I have enough of everything--and more than enough. My wants are fully satisfied now that I have received from the hands of Epaphroditus the generous gifts which you sent me--they are a fragrant odor, an acceptable sacrifice, truly pleasing to God." (Philippians 4:18, Weymouth)

14. GENEROSITY COMES FROM THE HEART OF GOD

"Every generous act of giving and every perfect gift is from above and comes down from the Father who made the heavenly lights, in whom there is no inconsistency or shifting shadow." (James 1:17, ISV)

15. GENEROSITY HAS OPENED UP THE WAY FOR YOUR PROSPERITY

"You know the generous grace of our Lord Jesus Christ. Though he was rich, yet for your sakes he became poor, so that by his poverty he could make you rich." (2 Corinthians 8:9, NLT)

16. GENEROSITY GIVEN AWAY CONTAINS THE POWER FOR GENEROUS MULTIPLICATION INTO YOUR LIFE

"Remember this: Whoever sows sparingly will also reap sparingly, and whoever sows generously will also reap generously." (2 Corinthians 9:6)

17. EVERY GENEROUS GIFT PLEASES THE HEART OF GOD

"Do not neglect to do good and to be generous, for God is pleased with such sacrifices." (Hebrews 13:16)

18. EXPECT GENEROSITY TO COME INTO YOUR LIFE FROM UNUSUAL SOURCES

"The Lord had made the Egyptians favorably disposed toward the people, and they gave them what they asked for; so they plundered the Egyptians." (Exodus 12:36)

19. GENEROSITY TOWARDS THE POOR HONORS THE LORD

"He who oppresses the poor shows contempt for their Maker, but whoever is kind to the needy honors God." (Proverbs 14:31)

20. GENEROSITY WILL CAUSE YOUR LIGHT TO SHINE IN THE DARKEST PLACES

"Light shines in the darkness for the godly. They are generous, compassionate, and righteous." (Psalm 112:4)

QUOTES ON GENEROSITY

- "I have held many things in my hands, and I have lost them all. But whatever I have placed in God's hands, that I still possess." ~Martin Luther, German reformer and theologian
- "If you haven't got any charity in your heart, you have the worst kind of heart trouble." ~Bob Hope, American comedian
- "If a person gets his attitude toward money straight, it will help straighten out almost every other area in his life." ~Billy Graham, American evangelist
- "We must make the invisible kingdom visible in our midst." ~John Calvin, French theologian and reformer

From the pages of this book I want to minister to you by the Spirit of God in regards to the three Realms of Generosity: **Blessing, Favor,** and **Increase.** Every opportunity to be generous is really an opportunity for you to experience God's blessing, favor, and increase in your own life!

Many times God works in threes: the Trinity, the Father Son and Holy Spirit. In the Spirit of God there are three realms of the supernatural: faith, anointing, and Glory (I have a fascinating teaching on this topic in **The Intensified Glory Institute® School Of Signs & Wonders, Course I).** We read about the three signs mentioned in Acts 2, blood, fire and smoke.

And of course, Jesus ministered for three years while he lived on the earth and He rose from the dead on the third day. The third day is the day of resurrection power and life! (I'm a third day kind of person, a person in the day of Glory, called for the Glory, born for the Glory, and made to reveal the Glory.) We are made in threes – a spirit with a soul that is housed in a body. As you can see throughout Scripture, God loves to work in threes.

In the next three chapters we will explore these three realms of generosity. As we do, I believe that you are going to receive a supernatural impartation for resurrection power to be released in your finances!   *No more Delay*

> *"Though one may be over powered, two can defend themselves but a cord of three strands is not quickly broken."* (Ecclesiastes 4:12)

There is a reason why God works in threes and a reason He sets into motion the three dimensions or the three realms of generosity: A three corded strand will not be broken. Somebody say, "I'm not going to be broke; God is bringing me into a realm of generosity!" Come on, you need to declare it! Say this out loud with me:

> *God is bringing me into a realm of generosity where I'm going to experience the greatest days of my life, for a cord of three strands is not quickly broken!*

CHAPTER FOUR

ℰXPERIENCING THE BLESSING

Honor the LORD with your wealth, with the firstfruits of all your crops; then your barns will be filled to overflowing, and your vats will brim over with new wine. ~Proverbs 3:9-10

As a young child my parents taught me to tithe to our local church. I guess I was blessed in this way because I never had to overcome any religious thinking or doubts about this financial matter. Whenever I received money through birthday gifts or Christmas presents, or from doing my weekly household chores, I would bring my tithe to Sunday School each week.

> *"I the LORD do not change. So you, the descendants of Jacob, are not destroyed. Ever since the time of your ancestors you have turned away from my decrees and have not kept them. Return to me, and I will return to you," says the LORD Almighty.*

"But you ask, 'How are we to return?'

"Will a mere mortal rob God? Yet you rob me.

"But you ask, 'How are we robbing you?'

"In tithes and offerings. You are under a curse— your whole nation—because you are robbing me. Bring the whole tithe into the storehouse, that there may be food in my house. Test me in this," says the LORD Almighty, "and see if I will not throw open the floodgates of heaven and pour out so much blessing that there will not be room enough to store it. I will prevent pests from devouring your crops, and the vines in your fields will not drop their fruit before it is ripe," says the LORD Almighty. "Then all the nations will call you blessed, for yours will be a delightful land," says the LORD Almighty. (Malachi 3:6-12)

The tithe has been established by God and it is set at 10 percent of what we receive. Some people ask the question about whether this is before or after taxes. It always amazes me how many Christians would like to get away with as much blessing as they can, for the littlest effort. Isn't this the fleshly nature? If you're already asking this question, then you're probably looking for some loop-hole in God's system of tithing. God says to bring the WHOLE tithe into the storehouse. That means 10 percent of everything that you have... all that you earn, all that you're gifted with, everything that comes into your hands! Just because the government has decided to take their share before it comes into your hands doesn't mean that 10 percent of that doesn't belong to God! Remember, we are supposed to pay our tithe first, before we pay for anything else.

> *Once when Jacob was cooking some stew, Esau came in from the open country, famished. He said to Jacob, "Quick, let me have some of that red stew! I'm famished!" (That is why he was also called Edom.)*
>
> *Jacob replied, "First sell me your birthright."*
>
> *"Look, I am about to die," Esau said. "What good is the birthright to me?"*
>
> *But Jacob said, "Swear to me first." So he swore an oath to him, selling his birthright to Jacob.*
>
> *Then Jacob gave Esau some bread and some lentil stew. He ate and drank, and then got up and left.*
>
> *So Esau despised his birthright.* (Genesis 25:29-34)

In the Scriptures we read the testimony of Jacob and Esau. It is an interesting story about the appetite of immediate desire and the willingness to let go of something precious in the "heat of the moment," but the end result in this story is that Esau sold Jacob his birthright for a bowl of soup! Can you imagine ever selling your inheritance for such a small menial thing? What a terrible trade. Sure, I know Esau was hungry and he didn't know what else to do. But surely there was something he could have done besides selling his birthright. His

God's work done in God's way will never lack God's supply. ~J. Hudson Taylor, English Missionary to China

birthright would have guaranteed him special authority within his family (next in line to his parents), a double-portion of inheritance, the Father's blessing and even the inheritance of the land of Canaan! I don't care how good your clam chowder tastes, none of this even comes close in comparison to a measly bowl of soup!

You know what amazes me though? I have met so many wonderful people who love the Lord and yet they haven't discovered the joy of honoring the Lord with their finances. Many of these people have a problem with the system of tithing. They think that the tithe is just an Old Testament regulation under the law, or that they should be able to decide what they want to give and when they want to give it. The problem with this kind of thinking is that it's contrary to the Word of God. Just like Esau made a terrible trade for his birthright, many Christians sell the blessing of God on their lives for a mere ten cents! I'm talking about ten cents out of every dollar!

There's no need to be the richest man in the cemetery. You can't do any business from there. ~Colonel Sanders, Founder of Kentucky Fried Chicken

If you think about this, it doesn't take much time to realize that if God asks for ten cents and tells you that you can keep the other ninety cents, that's a pretty nice deal! Especially, when God tells you that the ten cents represents your inheritance policy! God gives us the tithe with the obligation to pay it back to him in order for us to walk in a level of faith that connects us to the blessing. Faith connects us to the grace of God.

I like to compare the tithe to a rental car. I have rented hundreds of cars while traveling all over the world, but one time I rented a car in California and unfortunately the rental company never logged my return back into their computers. I was ministering in Virginia when I got a call from the rental company asking me to return the car. I tried to explain the situation to them, but because they didn't have any record of the return in their system, they told me that the police would be notified if the car wasn't returned within twenty-four hours!

A lot of people are willing to give God the credit, but not too many are willing to give Him the cash. ~Anonymous

You see, the whole idea of renting a car is to be able to use it for the allotted time and intended purpose, but in the end, return it back to where it came from. If you don't return the car, they will report you to the police and call you a thief!

Thankfully, over the next day this matter was sorted out and they discovered that I had indeed returned the car to them. The tithe is like a rental car. It is a gift from God intended to be returned to God with faith. God gives us the tithe in the first place to use for a specific purpose (that is, to present back to the Lord). And when we bring our tithes to the Lord in faith, it connects us to the blessings that have been provided to us through grace!

> *For it is by grace you have been saved, through faith--and this not from yourselves, it is the gift of God.* (Ephesians 2:8)

If we don't return the tithe to the Lord, the Word of God says that we are robbing God or stealing from Him (Malachi 3:8). In the same way, if I didn't return the rental car to the place where I got it, they would have called the police and reported me for theft!

People Of A New Covenant

Christ redeemed us from the curse of the law by becoming a curse for us, for it is written: "Cursed is everyone who is hung on a pole." (Galatians 3:13)

Tithing is not under the law, but it is a spiritual pattern. Tithing is a pattern of faith. Abraham understood this spiritual principle and he put it into practice by tithing to King Melchizedeck four hundred years before Moses and the law! We must understand that tithing wasn't a practice that came with the law, but it was a spiritual pattern that God had put into order from the days of Abraham. In the book of Romans we are encouraged as new covenant people to walk in the footsteps of the faith of Abraham (Romans 4:12).

If Abraham could be obedient to the Lord through paying his tithes to King Melchizedeck (and this king died thousands of years ago), how much more should we want to offer our 10 percent to King Jesus Christ who lives forever and provides us with the eternal gift of salvation! This is our better covenant (Hebrews 7:22). We don't pay our tithes to the dead, but we offer them with gratitude to the living!

"Woe to you, teachers of the law and Pharisees, you hypocrites! You give a tenth of your spices—mint,

dill and cumin. But you have neglected the more important matters of the law—justice, mercy and faithfulness. You should have practiced the latter, without neglecting the former." (Matthew 23:23)

Jesus spoke about the issue of tithing in the New Testament. He encouraged the new covenant believers to continue to do it. In speaking to the Pharisees, Jesus Christ rebuked them because they were offering their tithes without practicing genuine Christian love. As we worship the Lord with our finances, we need to make sure that we continue to walk in love. We can no longer afford to go through the motions (1 Corinthians 13:1). Faith mixed with love becomes an unstoppable force of blessing in the earth.

Four Scriptural Blessings For Tithing

The Bible tells us that there are four scriptural blessings for tithing. I want to share these with you and show you how being a tither can revolutionize your world by unlocking this realm of blessing over your life and connecting you to the supernatural flow of God's glory!

1. YOUR TITHE WILL ENSURE PROVISION OF SPIRITUAL FOOD

Bring the whole tithe into the storehouse, that there may be food in my house. Test me in this," says the LORD Almighty, "and see if I will not throw open the floodgates of heaven and pour out so much blessing that there will not be room enough to store it. (Malachi 3:10)

How many Christians have been sitting in their churches starving for real spiritual food; that is, the nutrients and goodness that comes from a rich meal in the Word of God? The Scriptures declare that your tithe will ensure a provision of spiritual food in the house of God. Your tithe belongs in your local church. It belongs wherever you are receiving your spiritual food. The reason why it belongs there is very practical. Your financial contributions will allow the bills to be paid, the ministries to function and give your Spiritual Leader the ability to focus on what God is saying, rather than trying to make sure that all ends meet! I can't tell you how many times I have ministered in churches where the Pastors needed to take two or three jobs on the side just to ensure that the lights could be turned on in the church and his family could eat and be provided for. This is so sad and it doesn't have to be this way.

I never would have been able to tithe the first million dollars I ever made if I had not tithed my first salary, which was $1.50 per week.
~John. D. Rockefeller, Sr., American Industralist and Philanthropist

When somebody has a call on their life to do the work of the ministry through the role of Pastor, Prophet, Evangelist, Teacher, or Apostolic Leader, their provision should come from those that they are encouraging spiritually (1 Timothy 5:17-18). It is my firm belief that the only reason why a Se-

nior Pastor would need to take on an additional job is because the people within the congregation are not tithers. The Bible says that if you tithe there will always be "food" or supernatural provision within the House of God. Your tithe guarantees a blessing in your life! Your tithe guarantees a blessing in the life of your church!

2. YOUR TITHE WILL CONNECT YOU TO AN OPEN HEAVEN

> *Bring the whole tithe into the storehouse, that there may be food in my house. Test me in this," says the LORD Almighty, "and see if I will not throw open the floodgates of heaven and pour out so much blessing that there will not be room enough to store it.* (Malachi 3:10)

The Bible says in the Old Testament that God would open up the windows of heaven if the people would bring their tithe. Now this was Old Testament law and we are no longer bound by this law, praise God! We have been set free from the curse of the law to live in supernatural victory for the rest of our lives through the finished work of Jesus Christ. We read in Scripture that when the veil in the temple was torn, it opened up the heavens. Jesus opened up the heavens for you and He's not going to close them again! Don't beg God to open the heavens; they are already open. But what are you doing about it?

The Bible tells us that even though all grace has been provided through Jesus, we must still reach out to receive this grace by faith (see Ephesians 2:8). When you begin to tithe (this means bringing 10 percent of your income to God), it opens up a supernatural dimension of blessing over your life, because it will connect you to the open heaven. Your tithe represents your faith in obedience. It always has and it always will. Finances will come to us right out of the "open windows of heaven" when we tithe. We won't be able to explain it because it will be so supernatural.

When I was ministering in Victoria, Canada, a few years ago, we began to see another kind of financial miracle that we had never experienced before. I received a call from our ministry office and they told me that our phone bills were coming into the office as a credit amount. In other words, the phone company was saying that they owed us money, not the usual other way around! We checked into this because we were certain that we had not paid too much money the month before, and sure enough this appeared to be a financial miracle of another kind.

As I was ministering at Victoria Miracle Center that week, I began to share the good news of this testimony and you could feel the spirit of faith beginning to rise in the atmosphere! To make a long story short, this miracle continued with us for several months with various office bills. Each month these bills would come back to us stating that we had a greater amount of credit on them. Instead of owing anything, it just seemed as though God was supernaturally paying our bills each month in an overflowing way! A few weeks after returning home from Victoria, the Pastors contacted me and told me that they too had begun experiencing this same financial miracle!

Your tithe connects you to the blessing. An act of faith connects you to the grace of God. An act of generosity connects you with the blessings that generosity brings!

The Bible says that as we begin walking in the glory through our tithing, it will not only connect us with the open windows of heaven and pour out a blessing in our finances, but it will even rebuke the devourer.

> *H*e does not possess wealth that allows it to possess him.
> ~Benjamin Franklin, American Inventor

3. YOUR TITHE IS A SPIRITUAL PESTICIDE!

"I will prevent pests from devouring your crops, and the vines in your fields will not drop their fruit before it is ripe," says the LORD Almighty. (Malachi 3:11)

A few years ago I was ministering in some outdoor revival tent meetings. The bugs were so bad that I wasn't sure how I was going to be able to finish my set of meetings as the people were itching, scratching and trying to swat away the mosquitoes almost constantly. During the second night of my ministry as I was in the pulpit preaching, suddenly I heard the voice of the Lord speak to me and say, *Joshua, don't you know that I can shut up the mouths of those mosquitoes just like I shut up the mouths of the lions for Daniel?* This was a revelation to me. I had never considered the possibility of God being able to move in this way before. So from the pulpit I began to speak what God had said to me. I declared that my meetings under the tent would be a "mosquito-free zone." Do you know what happened? This revelation from God began to work! All the bugs lifted in the tent, and even though they were still flying around the top of the tent, these mosquitoes did not come back down and bite anybody for the rest of my meetings under the tent. The Lord gave us a mosquito-free zone! In addition to these pests not being able to bite us anymore, those who had already been bitten began to receive instant miracles in their bodies as the swelling went down and the itching stopped. This was an amazing miracle from God!

Whatever you can walk away from, you have mastered. Tithing is the proof that you have mastered greed! ~Dr. Mike Murdock, Evangelist and Entrepreneur

These are the things that happen when you begin to walk in the glory through your tithe. Did you know that your tithe is a supernatural defense against the attacks of the enemy? It is your sign of authority over the works of the devil. Your tithe is a spiritual pesticide that will give you a "bug free" zone in your finances. We have seen this happen time and time again.

When you're a tither, there is a supernatural blessing that comes on your finances to rebuke the devourer. The enemy might try to attack your finances, but because you've given them to the Lord first by paying your tithe, there is a supernatural line of defense over your finances as you tithe. Psalm 84:11 shows true that *"the Lord is [your] sun and [your] shield."*

Several years ago I went directly to the local airport to purchase an airline ticket for an upcoming ministry trip. As the lady behind the counter told me how much the ticket was, I proceeded to hand her the exact amount, which was several hundreds of dollars in cash. She took all the money and walked away over to another counter. I was wondering why she was taking so long, and finally she called my sister and I over to her and began to tell us that I had forgotten to pay her a few hundred dollars for this ticket! I couldn't believe what my ears were hearing as I had handed her the exact amount needed to go on this particular flight. By the Spirit, I knew that this lady was attempting to pocket some of this money as I had handed her a large amount of cash.

The Bible says that if you're a tither, there is a spiritual pesticide on your money as the tithe will rebuke the devourer! The enemy can't take it because it doesn't belong to him; it belongs to God! As I stood in front of the counter, I began to pray in tongues and it looked like the lady behind the counter was getting nervous. She didn't know what I was going to do!

The Dead Sea is the dead sea because it continually receives and never gives. ~Anonymous

At that moment, my sister looked down on the floor in front of the counter (now this was down further from where we had originally paid for the ticket). The exact money that we needed was sitting on the floor in front of us as several hundred dollars were scattered around. As we picked up that money and handed it to the lady, her face appeared as though she had seen a ghost! I believe that God took that money right out of her pocket and put it on the other side of the counter in front of us because that money belonged to God! Needless to say, we received the airline ticket and walked away praising the Lord for His faithfulness to us!

There is a supernatural line of defense around your finances as you tithe! People may try to rob you or rip you off, but when you are a tither, you are blessed!

4.   PEOPLE WILL CALL YOU BLESSED!

> *"Then all the nations will call you blessed, for yours will be a delightful land," says the LORD Almighty.* (Malachi 3:12)

As we trust God first before anything else and we pay our tithes, others around us are not going to understand how we remain blessed. Some may have the same jobs and live on the same income, but when we pay our tithes the Bible says that others will call us blessed! I want to be called blessed, don't you? You can be blessed in the middle of an economic recession because your faith is not based on an economy built by man. Our financial provision and supply come directly from the true riches in heavenly glory! Your tithe has the ability to increase, expand and multiply your finances with blessing because you have completely committed them to the Lord.

No one has ever become poor by giving. ~Anne Frank, Jewish Dutch Diarist During Nazi Occupation

> *And my God will meet all your needs according to the riches of his glory in Christ Jesus.* (Philippians 4:19)

You can be blessed when it looks like financial devastation and there isn't enough to go around because Jesus Christ multiplied the loaves and fish! He doesn't need a lot to accomplish a lot! His name is El Shaddai; He is the Lord of more than enough!

> *So Abraham called that place The LORD Will Provide. And to this day it is said, "On the mountain of the LORD it will be provided."* (Genesis 22:14)

If these scriptural blessings for tithing were available under the law, how much more blessing and glory will we see as we allow the pattern of tithing to become a part of our lives as new covenant believers! Moses experienced a fading glory, but we are walking into a realm of blessing where an ever-increasing glory comes upon us in our finances.

We pay our tithes. We don't pray about what we are supposed to tithe because we are told through the Scriptures that our tithe is equal to 10 percent of all of our income. This is what we must pay to God. It is an act of obedience and represents our faith in action.

I am blessed because I am a tither! You can be too!

Prayer For Unlocking The Realm Of Blessing

"Father, right now in the name of Jesus, I purpose in my hearts to be a tither into Your kingdom. As I step into Your blessings through this act of faith, I step into the cloud of Your Glory. I enter into that supernatural dimension of blessing that connects me with the open floodgates of heaven over my life. I believe that right now You are releasing Angelic hosts to minister on my behalf. Lord, I thank You for the open heaven that's filled with rare treasure and unusual riches.

"I believe that Your blessings are being released into my life because I'm a tither and I'm coming into alignment with the truth of Your Word. I thank You that a spiritual pesticide is being released over my life today. Every place where the enemy has tried to steal, kill and destroy, Your supernatural protection is filling those places. Blessings are coming to me with divine encounters, heavenly wisdom, unusual means of provision, and Your revelation. I believe that others will look at me and call me blessed because Your glory is shining through my life. Thank You, Lord, for this amazing opportunity You have given me to participate with heavenly blessings. In Jesus' name. Amen."

CHAPTER FIVE

SUPERNATURAL FAVOR

"Give, and it shall be given unto you; good measure, pressed down, and shaken together, and running over, shall men give into your bosom. For with the same measure that ye mete withal it shall be measured to you again." ~Luke 6:38, KJV

I have discovered an amazing connection between our financial offerings and the divine favor of God. I am not saying that you can buy your miracle or work for God's favor. You cannot do that. However, throughout the Scriptures people positioned their lives to receive generously from the Lord as they aligned their hearts with the heart of God. We serve a generous God and He wants us to connect with that reality.

As I have shared before, everything you will ever need has already been made available to you through the finished work of Jesus Christ on the cross of Calvary. It is a finished work. But it is your faith in that finished work that connects you to the tangible realities of the grace of God. It is necessary for you to appropriate these blessings in order to receive the favor of God in your life.

I have met many people around the world who are struggling every day in the area of finances. They refuse to tithe and they refuse to give financial offerings. Each one of them is loved by God, and He has already made every blessing available to them. But the question remains, *Why are they not prospering?* Do they have *information* or do they have *revelation* about God's desire to bless their life? Information is useless without a revelation. Information can cause you to argue until you're blue in the face and still lack results. But a revelation will cause you to move towards an activation in order to produce a manifestation of the information! God's revelation will always motivate you towards generosity.

> *N*o person was ever honored for what he received. Honor has been the reward for what he gave. ~Calvin Coolidge, 30th President of the United States

> *The people rejoiced over the offerings, for they had given freely and wholeheartedly to the Lord, and King David was filled with joy.* (1 Chronicles 29:9, NLT)

In the Old Testament, David was delighted by watching the people give so willingly to the Lord. How much more as New Covenant believers should we seek to give freely to the Lord. When you truly understand the heart of God, you will be motivated to pursue this realm of God's glory.

The connection between generous giving and the divine presence of God's favor is obvious within the Scriptures. I believe, as Christians, that our giving should flow from the generous heart of God. It is this offering that connects us to the realization that we serve an amazing God who cannot be outdone in His extravagance. Look at these examples throughout Scripture:

- God's first instruction to Moses for building the tabernacle in the wilderness was to receive an offering for the Shekinah Glory to reside within that atmosphere (Exodus 25:1-9).

- Paul told the Philippian Church that when their generous offerings were given to the Lord as a fragrance that it would cause God to respond and release the supply for their areas of need (Philippians 4:14-19).

- Great power and grace was released to the early church as they gave generously at the feet of the Apostles (Acts 4:32-35).

So you may wonder... how is the offering different from the tithe? An offering is something that God requests and we give. Offerings come in all shapes and sizes. It's not set at 10 percent like the tithe. Sometimes offerings are little and other times they are huge, but the key here is that God sets the offering. Contrary to popular belief, we don't decide the offering, but God decides. Consider the following story of Cain and Abel.

Now Abel kept flocks, and Cain worked the soil. In the course of time Cain brought some of the fruits of the soil as an offering to the Lord. But Abel brought fat portions from some of the firstborn of his flock. The

Lord looked with favor on Abel and his offering, but on Cain and his offering he did not look with favor. So Cain was very angry, and his face was downcast. Then the Lord said to Cain, "Why are you angry? Why is your face downcast? If you do what is right, will you not be accepted? But if you do not do what is right, sin is crouching at your door; it desires to have you, but you must master it." (Genesis 4:2-6)

Cain and Abel both presented their offerings to God, but the Scriptures tell us that God refused to receive Cain's offering, but He looked with favor on Abel and his offering. Why did this happen? God rejected Cain's offering because it was given in self-will and unbelief. Offerings must always be done in faith.

By faith Abel offered God a better sacrifice than Cain did. By faith he was commended as a righteous man, when God spoke well of his offerings. (Hebrews 11:4)

How does faith come? How can we present an offering to God in faith? Faith comes by hearing, and hearing by the Word of God (Romans 10:17). This is why it's so important to hear the voice of God about the offerings that you give. God always sets the offering. He speaks, we hear, and we're supposed to give our offerings in faith. We must listen to the revelation and then be obedient to it (James 1:22).

All the believers were one in heart and mind. No one claimed that any of his possessions was his own, but they shared everything they had. With great power the apostles continued to testify to the resurrection of the Lord Jesus, and much grace was upon them all. There were no needy persons among them. For from time to time those who owned lands or houses sold them, brought the money from the sales and put it at the apostles' feet, and it was distributed to anyone as he had need. (Acts 4:32-35)

As all the believers were one in heart and mind, the new covenant church in Acts 4 was given very specific instructions from the Lord. The precedent was given to tithe 10 percent and give 90 percent offerings to the work of the gospel. This was the standard that the Lord set for them at that time. They put everything they had into the work of the Lord by selling their land, homes, and other valuables in order to lay them at the apostles' feet. They did it with gladness and a spirit of generosity.

If we read further into the book of Acts, we will discover that there were two people in this community who did not obey the divine instructions that were given for the offering. Ananias and Sapphira actually lied about their offering by keeping a portion and giving the remainder (Acts 5:1-5). According to Malachi 3:8 it is possible to rob God of the offerings, not just the tithe. If we are not obedient to His voice, then we rob Him and we rob

There are always two people on the other side of your giving. Those who receive the gift and those who pour back gifts into your life! ~Joshua Mills

ourselves of connecting with the fullness of His favor upon our lives.

Quite a few years ago the Lord spoke to me about going to Brazil. Just a few weeks after the Lord put that desire on my heart, I received a call from a Pastor asking me to come! It has always happened this way for us. The Lord will give us a burden for a specific nation, we will lay hands on the map and pray and thank the Lord for opening up the door, and within just a month or two we will generally receive a supernatural connection to go and minister there.

Anyway, this Pastor in Belo Horizonte, Brazil, asked me to come and minister in the springtime of the following year. We set some dates and I asked him to call back in a few months to confirm all the arrangements for the venue and ministry details. But after several attempts to communicate through phone and email, I didn't hear back from that Pastor until two weeks before I was supposed to arrive into Brazil. I had assumed other plans had been made and that he no longer desired to have me come to his church. I was wrong! He called and told me about the advertising he had done, the churches he had lined up, and the great time we were going to have when I came to minister in Belo Horizonte!

The measure of a life is not its duration, but its donation. ~Peter Marshall, Former U.S. Senate Chaplain

Well praise God, this was wonderful, except for the fact that it was only two weeks before departure and I didn't have any money to pay for an airline ticket to Brazil! I called my travel agent and asked her to find me the lowest airfare to Brazil. She called back and said it was $2,500! Where was I going to get that kind of money in the next few days?

Janet Angela and I went to prayer about it and the Lord gave us a peace. Within the following days we filed our year-end income taxes with a local accountant and we realized that our income tax return was going to be just over $2,500! Hallelujah! Even though we needed that money to pay for other bills, we committed it to the Lord. We paid our tithes from that money and the rest we used for missions as we invested it into this trip to Brazil. God has a way to work miracles for you! Even when you don't see the light at the end of the tunnel – He is the light! And He will shine in your darkest night!

> *Giving opens up the gate for unlimited favor to flow into your life. ~Joshua Mills*

A few weeks later as Janet Angela was taking me to the airport to go on this trip, Lincoln was crying in the back seat and Janet Angela was crying as she was driving the car because I was leaving for two weeks and she didn't have any money to pay for the bills. I remember a spirit of faith rising up in me because I knew that God wouldn't call me into the nations and leave my family desolate as I traveled.

We had paid our tithes and given our offerings in obedience to the Lord! We had a promise from the Word of God and I was holding onto it for dear life! When everything else goes wrong, the Word of God will always be right. You've got to hang on to those precious Scriptures when it doesn't make sense in the natural, and when it seems as though all hope is gone. God's Word will always work if you believe it.

That morning we had some bills that needed to be paid, things that needed to be taken care of in the ministry, and I didn't have any extra spending money to take with me on the trip. But God had told me to go to Brazil. The truth is when you have favor on your life, you don't have to worry how it's all going to work out. You must do your part and allow God to do His.

Give me five minutes with a person's checkbook, and I will tell you where their heart is." ~Billy Graham, American Evangelist

So we were driving to the airport without any money in our hands or in our bank accounts, and I remember we began to pray in the car. I asked Janet Angela, *"How much money do you need to pay our bills when I am gone?"* and she said, *"We need $1,000."* And so I said, *"Okay, let's just believe God together that He's just going to give us the $1,000 that we need. I don't know how it's going to come to us, but we have the Lord's favor on our lives and I know it's going to come."*

The Bible says that if we've given our offerings to God then it's going to be given back to us. I've heard somebody say, "When you take care of God's business, He takes care of yours." And so we finished praying in the car and Janet Angela dropped me off at the airport for my two week ministry trip to Brazil.

As I was leaving on the airplane, Janet Angela went to the mailbox and found a letter in the mail with a $1,000 check! This was exactly what we needed and it came all the way from the Canadian Arctic! Even before we prayed, God had already set His answer into motion. I believe that our offerings had prepared the groundwork with a divine intervention of favor! The Lord had spoken to that dear Inuit man about sending us that exact amount of money, and as he obeyed the Lord, he became a catalyst for the miracle!

Your offerings will connect you with supernatural favor! That $1,000 check came from a place that we would have never expected! But this is what favor will do for you – provision will come from unusual places of supply! Your generous offering positions you for generous favor!

We have never sought riches out of a materialistic desire for greed. As I told you before, we have learned how to live with both less and with more. But we have discovered that this principle of giving always works. The more we desire to bless the Lord and give

When it comes to giving until it hurts, most people have a very low threshold of pain. ~Anonymous

ourselves fully to the eternal work of His kingdom, we have found ourselves connecting with the reality that He is the King of Glory and He desires to shower good gifts on His children!

So you're wondering... how does this all work? We don't pay offerings (they are not a repayment of a loan God has given to us, like the tithe). We always give our offerings. The Bible says that God loves a cheerful and prompt-to-do-it giver whose heart is in the giving. So we should always bring our offerings to God with a happy heart and cheerful spirit. We need to put everything we are into our offerings!

Do you realize that it's absolutely impossible to out-give God? It's a simple truth, but I've discovered that God's hands are much bigger than mine. When I give to Him, He gives back much more. Let's look at the scriptural proof. According to Luke 6:38 being obedient in our giving opens up at least seven levels of supernatural receiving! I've been able to experience all seven of these levels in my own personal life as I have followed the principle of giving and receiving!

7 LEVELS OF SUPERNATURAL RECEIVING

"Give, and it will be given to you. A good measure, pressed down, shaken together and running over, will be poured into your lap. For with the measure you use, it will be measured to you." (Luke 6:38)

Many people have read this Scripture verse from the Word of God and thought that this was a revelation about giving. Actually, this beautiful passage of Scripture is all about receiving! There is only one mention of giving in the entire verse, but there are several notable revelations about receiving the blessings from God.

According to this verse, we can find that there are seven supernatural levels of receiving that can be achieved from your willingness to give. Your gift will always make a way for you and create the spark that ignites unlimited spheres of favor in your life. Here are these seven levels that are created through the generous act of giving.

1.   IT WILL BE GIVEN BACK TO YOU

In the first level of receiving, you will begin to receive back what you have given away. Janet Angela and I have experienced this level many times in our life. Often we have given in to other people's lives by paying for their meals or offering to take them to a nice place to eat. It's amazing how many times people have done the same for us!

Several years ago I went to India, and while I was visiting the construction site of an orphanage, I felt led of the Lord to give my brand-new Fossil watch to a worker who was at the site. He was so blessed! He could hardly

As your hands are outstretched to give your palms become opened in a greater position to receive. ~Joshua Mills

believe that I would do such a thing for him! Well, I can't tell you how many times I have received watches as a gift! I love watches – they are something I love to collect and wear, and now I have an ample supply because I was willing to give one away!

Just recently as I was ministering in Brisbane, Australia, my evangelist friend Chris Harvey turned to me in the meeting and showed me his beautiful TAG watch with eleven diamonds on it. He asked me if I liked it, and I responded with a resounding *"Yes!"* He then proceeded to give it to me right there in the meeting! I felt so blessed and overwhelmed by the goodness of God because this watch was much more nicer than any other watch I had ever owned before. This takes us to the next level of receiving...

2. GOOD MEASURE

The second level of receiving is the ability to receive not only what you've given away – but tapping into the realm of God's supply where you experience the "good measure." The TAG watch that I received as a gift in Australia was a good measure. It was a better measure than I had originally given away! It amazes me that no matter how much we give or how generous we become, we will never be able to out-give God! *It's a simple truth that God's hands are bigger than mine!*

3. PRESSED DOWN

I want pressed down prosperity! I mean, I want my life to be filled to capacity with the blessings of God so that I can release these blessings to others. Wealth is intended to be used for God's kingdom, not for greed or selfish reasons. This is the simple reason why God wants to bless you with a pressed down level of favor!

4. SHAKEN TOGETHER

This level of receiving from God often requires us to let go of trivial things so that God can impart more important and meaningful blessings into our life. We must let go of our poverty so that we can grab hold of His prosperity. We must let go of our pain, so that we can obtain His peace. We must let go of old mindsets so that we can become God-minded in our un-

understanding of Kingdom economics. I believe that God wants to shake us, and rid us of anything that would not be of Him, while at the same time filling us to the maximum capacity with His goodness and His life!

5. RUNNING OVER

I have come to realize that God wants to give us a blessing so big that we are unable to contain it! I like this level of receiving! This is the place of overflow and abundance! In Psalm 23:5, the Psalmist David sang that he had been anointed with oil and that his cup overflowed! Wouldn't you like to be able to sing that song too? The Lord desires for you to tap into this fifth level of receiving where your cup of prosperity overflows with the goodness of God!

6. OTHERS WILL POUR INTO YOUR LIFE

There are always two people on the other side of your giving: Those who will receive the gift and those who will pour back with gifts. Your offering assigns somebody to pour back into your life. In the King James translation it says *"shall men give into your bosom."* In other words, you will have favor with both God and men as you pay your tithes and give your offerings. Specifically

Giving is faith reaching to receive. ~Joshua Mills

the Bible says that men (and women) will give unto you by pouring abundance into your lap (into your bank accounts, into your home, into your ministry, etc.) when you are faithful to give your offerings as directed by the Lord.

7. WITH THE MEASURE YOU USE, IT WILL BE MEASURED TO YOU

Some people have given to God in a limited measure and always seem to be experiencing limited favor. The Bible makes it clear that we can determine "the measure" we experience in our life. If you want to go to new levels of receiving, you must begin to change your levels of giving! How would you like for a golden dump truck to open up over your life with remarkable blessings and divine appointments? You must begin pouring out to the degree you would like to receive!

Do you see how the realms build upon each other? We establish ourselves in the blessings of God with our tithes, but then when we give our offerings it takes us to whole new levels of favor. Not just with God, but also with men and women. Our offerings connect us to kingdom connections!

> *A gift opens the way for the giver and ushers him into the presence of the great.* (Proverbs 18:16)

The Bible says that a man's gift will make a way for him. Your giving will open up doors of opportunity, doors of expansion, doors of success and promotion. Your gift will open up doors of supernatural favor wherever you go.

Right now, ask the Lord to show you three places where you can give a financial offering today (it may be a ministry, church or missions organization, or even possibly your next-door neighbor). Right now let God show you what offering amount you're supposed to give. You may need to drive down the street, put it into the mail, or go online to give, but right now I want you to write down the names and gift amount:

monthly

1. _Keith Moore_ _____ Amount $ _10.00_
2. _Carl Britson_ Potts to lunch Amount $ _20.00_
3. _____ Amount $_____

As you give these offerings to God (by dispersing them into the places He has directed), begin to expect for men and women to show up in your life who will show you extreme favor! On earth our financial offerings are received by others so they can do the work of God. But in heaven those same generous offerings are received as a spiritual fragrance that delights the nostrils of the Lord! Begin focusing on the Scriptures found in chapter 11 and declare the will of God – that there are seven supernatural levels of favor opening up for you right now in Jesus' name!

Prayer For Unlocking The Realm Of Favor

"Father, right now in the name of Jesus, I step into that realm… I step into Your favor, I step into the cloud of Your Glory. I enter into the mist of miracles. I enter into that heavenly mist of signs and wonders and supernatural abundance; I step into the cloud of Kingdom wealth. Oh Jesus, You be glorified, You be exalted, You be lifted high in my life so that favor flows like a river. Let it flow like oil from your throne. Let Your favor flow like a shower of golden power. God I receive all that You have.

"I open myself to the heavens. I open up myself to the realm of Your Spirit so that I receive all that You have for me, in Jesus' mighty name. Kingdom prosperity in the land, favor opening up the door, favor opening up opportunities, favor opening up new ideas, even changing mind sets, favor rearranging thinking, favor downloading inventions and creative ideas, favor coming as a blueprint for success. Favor coming with Divine supernatural wisdom, guidance, understanding and revelation, in Jesus' mighty name."

Remember that whenever there is an opportunity to give, it really is an opportunity for you to show favor and for you to be favored. God loves your generosity. It causes His glory to come with supernatural blessing and favor. Say this with me: *I am favored because I am a giver!*

that if his seed doesn't produce successfully in one field, then surely it will bring increase in another field of fertile soil.

We are coming into a day where the reaper WILL overtake the sower!

> *"The days are coming," declares the LORD, "when the reaper will be overtaken by the plowman and the planter by the one treading grapes. New wine will drip from the mountains and flow from all the hills."*
> (Amos 9:13)   — Mine —

> *"Don't you have a saying, 'It's still four months until harvest'? I tell you, open your eyes and look at the fields! They are ripe for harvest. Even now the one who reaps draws a wage and harvests a crop for eternal life, so that the sower and the reaper may be glad together. Thus the saying 'One sows and another reaps' is true. I sent you to reap what you have not worked for. Others have done the hard work, and you have reaped the benefits of their labor."* (John 4:35-38)

I am a harvester because I am a sower!

The Merriam-Webster Online Dictionary says that the verb "sow" firstly means *"to plant seed for growth, especially by scattering"* and secondly this word means to *"set something in motion."* [3]

I like that the dictionary says that our sowing is *"setting something in motion"!* When we sow our financial seeds, we are setting ourselves into the motion of the glory. We simply begin moving into the flow of God's realm for increase. In the book of Jeremiah (29:11) the Bible says, *"For I know the plans I have for you, declares the Lord, plans to prosper you..."* As we sow to the heavens, we begin moving ourselves into the promises of God's supernatural provision. As we sow today, we begin setting in motion our harvest for tomorrow! Our seed moves us closer to our future. The furthest distance between you and your harvest is simply your seed!

We are rich only through what we give: and poor only through what we refuse and keep. ~Anne Swetchine, Russian-French Writer

The dictionary also gives us an understanding that as we sow, we should be planting our seed for growth, especially by scattering. What does this mean?

Whenever the farmer plans for his coming harvest, he always makes sure that he plants more than enough seed into the ground. He doesn't say, "I want one hundred bean plants, so I guess I'll just plant one hundred bean seeds." When he is preparing to sow his seed for harvest, He scatters his seeds in great abundance. The farmer is never quite sure which seed will grow into the harvest or which one will fall to the side and not produce a crop. This is why we must scatter our seed when we are unlocking this realm of increase in our life. We know that the harvest is coming, but we never quite know which one of our financial seeds might bring forth the greatest return!

Seed and Alms

Every day the Holy Spirit will set opportunities before us to plant seeds into good and fertile soil. Sometimes you may be walking down the street and be approached by the poor or needy that require your assistance. Instead of brushing these aside, begin seeing them as God does. When Jesus Christ was walking on the earth, He always had great compassion for all of mankind. Now as we've been given His shoes to wear, we are called to be those who will show great compassion to the poor. The Bible says that as we sow our alms to the poor, we are lending to the Lord.

> *He who has pity on the poor lends to the Lord, and He will pay back what he has given.* (Proverbs 19:17)

Within the context of Scripture, "alms" is another word for seed in relation to the less fortunate of our society. Alms are given as charity to benefit the poor. The poor cannot repay – we don't expect them too. We sow and release our alms to the poor, but then the Bible says that it is God that will repay us as we sow our seed. Some translations say that God will reward us! As we sow to the heavens, God begins sowing to the earth!

Many times the Lord has given us countless opportunities to sow into the mission field. We've donated thousands of Bibles throughout the Canadian Arctic, financially supported native outreaches in Sierra Leone, sponsored children in Thailand, as well as labored among the poor in Haiti, Mexico, and other parts of the world. We've never expected a return from the people we've met in those places, but we've always received a spiritual return from the Lord!

This is the nature of our seed!

Religion pure and undefiled with the God and Father is this, to look after orphans and widows in their tribulation. (James 1:27, Young's Literal Translation)

The Bible speaks about sowing our alms into orphans and widows. You may have an opportunity even right now to take care of an elderly woman or some desperate children in your church, community or family. Don't see this situation as a heavy burden, but rather begin to look at these opportunities as a realm that's being opened for you to move into the increase! The seed is in your hand, but the harvest is in God's hand! Your seed is useless without soil, and that is why God is placing these sowing opportunities all around us in this day! God desires for you to live in the increase of His harvest!

Sacrificial Sowing

Gather my saints together to Me, those who have made a covenant with Me by sacrifice. (Psalm 50:5, NKJV)

There are times when the Lord will present us with a need that seems almost too big, but do you realize that your seed is always bigger than your need when it's planted in the ground? This is the power of your seed.

Sometimes as we're learning to sow our seed it feels like a sacrifice because we're letting go of everything we have in our hand. This can be a difficult thing to do because it requires faith believing that the power within our seed for the future is greater than the present need we have today.

I remember the first time that I began to perceive what God could do with a seed. I was employed as an art instructor and was making only $35 a week at my job. I guess you could have called me a "starving artist" at that time. One afternoon at church I began to receive the revelation of what my seed could do as I heard the preacher speaking the Word of God (since *faith comes by hearing, and hearing by the word of God* - Romans 10:17).

You need to get around people who will speak faith into your life. Don't subject yourself to an atmosphere of doubt and unbelief because it will attempt to uproot your seeds and destroy your harvest. As I sat under the sound of God's Word, I knew in my spirit that what I was hearing was the truth. Remember, I was only making $35 a week at my job. I had a total of $60 in my wallet and I wanted to begin trying this new concept out, so I planted a $20 bill as my financial seed that afternoon. I felt like it was a sacrifice because I made so little at my job, but at the same time I was so excited to begin operating in this new way of living.

> *He who bestows his goods upon the poor shall have as much again, and ten times more. ~John Bunyan, English Author*

That night I returned to the meeting once again and dropped $40 into the bucket as a seed for harvest. This was an even bigger sacrifice because this was all I had left! I had already paid my tithes and I had given as the Lord instructed in the offerings, but now I was beginning to plant my seeds for increase!

Within a very short time, the Lord took me from that place of making only $35 a week to making $300 a week. Maybe this doesn't seem like such a big miracle to you, but for me, this was life changing! My weekly income increased almost nine times and I began to see other miracles begin to happen as well. Because I recognized the anointing that was on that preacher with my seed, I began to reap a harvest of anointing on my own life.

Do you want to receive an impartation of fresh miracle anointing in your life? If you do, it's important to sow into fertile soil and good ground. Find a ministry that is flowing in the things of God – I mean really moving in the gifts of the Spirit with a demonstration of miracles, signs and wonders, and sow your seed in that place on purpose. Expect to receive a financial harvest with an overflow of supernatural miracles!

Since that time my faith has been growing as I've exercised what the Lord has given to me. Some people say that they would be generous to sow if the Lord gave them $1,000 tomorrow, but if you're not able to let go of your $100 seed today, you certainly won't let go of $1,000 seed tomorrow. Let go of what's inside of your hand and God will let go of what's inside of His hand!

A man there was, and they called him Mad; the more he gave, the more he had. ~John Bunyan, English Author

With this increase of faith, Janet Angela and I have increased our seed on several occasions. I can remember the first time we were able to sow in the hundreds. This was so exciting because we realized the more seed we scattered, the greater the results of our harvest would be! God took us from that place and we walked into a harvest of increase where we were able to sow $1,000. I will never forget that night when we wrote that check because it seemed like we were living a dream!

It was our hearts' desire to sow a large amount into the work of the ministry. And because we were faithful to sow the $20 years before, God had brought us into a place of increase where we could sow $1,000. We rejoiced that night and felt such joy as we planted our seed into the glory! Since that time we've been able to sow hundreds of thousands of dollars, and now we're looking forward to the day when we can sow millions! We know that day is coming because with every seed comes an appointed harvest.

You can't purchase spiritual gifts with your money, but you can certainly use your finances to enter into that heavenly pattern of sowing and reaping. You've sown your dollars and cents into restaurants, shopping malls, entertainment facilities and countless household bills where your return has been limited to the earthly goods and services that they offer. What better place to invest your finances than in the glory realm. This is the atmosphere of heaven, where nothing is impossible with God, but all things are possible!

There is something addictive about becoming a generous giver! Once you break through into this revelation about blessing, favor and increase, you'll realize that there is no better way to live!

Our financial seed brings us into a financial covenant with God for financial increase. Every seed produces after its kind.

This is a natural and supernatural law that God has set into motion. If you sow seeds of finances, you will reap a harvest of finances. If you sow seeds of friendship, you will reap a harvest of friendship. Whatever seeds you sow will always determine the harvest that you will reap. It would be foolish for the farmer to expect a harvest of corn if he's only planted watermelon seeds. In the same way, it would be foolish for you to expect a harvest of financial increase if you haven't placed any financial seeds in the fertile soil of the glory realm.

> *"While the earth remains, seedtime and harvest, cold and heat, winter and summer, and day and night shall not cease."* (Genesis 8:22, NKJV)

As long as the earth remains, there will be seedtime and harvest. It's possible to count the apples on an apple tree, but it's impossible to count the apple trees within an apple seed. As your spirit begins to connect with this revelation about sowing and reaping, you will begin to realize that the possibilities for increase are endless!

It's possible to count the apples on an apple tree, but it's impossible to count the apple trees within an apple seed. ~Joshua Mills

God doesn't give us a seed so that we will eat it. How nourishing and satisfying would it be to eat your seed? It wouldn't be satisfying at all! And yet many Christians are trying to get by, living from paycheck to paycheck, debt to debt, and disappointment to disappointment. We must understand that God will give us seed so that we can sow it into the ground. Look at what 2 Corinthians 9:10 says:

Now he who supplies seed to the sower and bread for food will also supply and increase your store of seed and will enlarge the harvest of your righteousness.

God will supply seed and increase your store of seed... and if that's not enough, He will enlarge the harvest of your righteous. But there's more.

You will be enriched in every way so that you can be generous on every occasion, and through us your generosity will result in thanksgiving to God.

Did you see that? You will be enriched in *every* way on *every* occasion. The sacrificial sowing we were talking about doesn't seem so sacrificial anymore. And there's still more. Verse 12 goes on to say that not only will your giving be a blessing to meet the needs of God's people, but will also overflow in *many* expressions of thanks to God, which I believe includes thanks to God from those who do not yet know Christ. No wonder why this passage of Scripture ends with "Thanks be to God for his indescribable gift!" (See 2 Corinthians 9:6-15.)

God wants to take you from glory to glory! These small seeds today will result in an increase of fruits for tomorrow! In this day we must learn how to sow, for as we're faithful with the little, God will increase us in much!

Miracle Money Appearing

When Janet Angela and I were first married we lived on a very limited budget in the natural. I remember one week in particular when we had $15 left to our name. We were living and ministering in San Diego, California, at that time. We needed to put food on the table, we had to pay the electric bill and the phone bill. We also had to put gas in our car because we had to drive to church three times that week to minister (and it was a 30-minute drive each way). We didn't know what we were going to do. At that time we lived penny to penny, and just when we thought we weren't going to be able to make it, God would supply for us in the most unusual ways.

I was at church one night just praising the Lord and a wonderful peace came over me. The Bible says that God will give you peace even in the middle of a storm! In the natural, you might be facing the worst financial crisis you've ever known, but in the middle of it you can have a peace that passes all understanding. You might be facing bankruptcy, foreclosure, repossession or insurmountable debt, but the Lord can give you a peace in the middle of it. He alone can give you a way out, even where there seems to be no way out. *Don't ever stop believing for a miracle because God is always able to work one for you.*

That night in church Janet Angela and I gave everything we had into the offering. We were trusting God. We had no other way to make ends meet. At the end of the meeting my friend Paul asked me if I had some spare change for a soda because he needed just a few more cents. Almost out of instinct, I reached into my pocket to see if I had any coins left. To my surprise I felt something inside my pocket! It felt like paper money! I was startled to think that I may have had another dollar left to my name! You know, when you're so poor because you're living from penny to penny, a dollar in the pocket feels really good! I excitedly pulled this money from my pocket, but amazingly it wasn't a dollar bill, it was $100! I was dumbfounded. How did

$100 get into my pocket? There was no natural explanation for this money.

Janet Angela and I began rejoicing because of God's goodness to us! We knew that this miracle was directly from heaven. We believed that God had supernaturally placed that money into my pocket. As we had been faithful to do our part, He was faithful to do His. Because of this miracle we were able to pay some of our bills and take care of our expenses for the week. This gave us new insight into the realms of supernatural prosperity and motivated us more than ever in our pursuit of truth concerning God's kingdom economics.

The world asks, "What does a man own?" Christ asks, "How does he use it? ~Andrew Murray, South African Evangelist

Several years later, we witnessed this same kind of miracle for the multiplication of money as we were hosting our very first conference in Canada. In the book *I Serve The God Of Miracles* we had read the testimony about Rev. Edith Heflin counting the nightly offerings after the revivial meetings. As she persisted in prayer for the Lord to increase the finances, she would experience the multiplication of the offering so that all the bills could be paid in the ministry. Did you know that your testimony is filled with the prophetic ability to establish the purposes of God on earth? The Bible says that "the testimony of Jesus Christ is the spirit of prophecy" (Revelation 19:10). So just as we had read within the pages of that wonderful book, Janet Angela and I began to raise our nightly offerings to the Lord and ask for Him to multiply them for the work of the ministry. We knew that if God could do this miracle for the Heflins, He would be able to do it for us as well.

After praying over the offerings, Janet Angela and I began to count them for a second time, and would you believe that it seemed as though the money had multiplied as our faith had contended for this realm of financial increase. In amazement, we began to count the offerings again to make sure that we had counted them correctly. As we counted these finances over and over again, each time the money would multiply and we would have a larger total in the end. Finally after we had tallied the offerings four times, the money settled at an amount that would enable us to pay for all of our conference expenses. We took the money to the bank and praised the Lord because He is Jehovah Jireh, our Supernatural Provider!

When you begin to experience miracles like this in the area of your finances, it causes faith to arise within you. But as you share your testimony, it also releases an expectation into the atmosphere for God to do it in the lives of "whosoever will." Whenever God asks for us to give a specific offering, we will do it without hesitation because we've learned that there is always another miracle on the other side of our obedience (Deuteronomy 28). As we have shared these truths with thousands of people around the world, we have received testimony after testimony confirming that God is true to His Word.

Money is a great treasure that only increases as you give it away. ~Lord Francis Bacon, English Scientist

During our Summer Campmeeting in 2004, as I was ministering the truth of God's Word concerning financial stewardship, the realms of Glory opened with the possibility for money multiplication once again. Many people began to get out of their seats, running towards the altar area, cheerfully desiring to sow into the Glory realm.

Our tithes, offerings and seed should always be presented to the Lord with a cheerful spirit and happiness of heart. As these people gave into the offering, many began to experience money multiplying in their pockets, purses, wallets and even within the pages of their Bibles! Several people began to share testimonies about the Lord multiplying the last of their monies and causing new $20 bills, $50 bills and even $100 bills to appear where there had been no money previously! I remember that at least 10 different people had experienced the multiplication of $20 bills that night. It was astonishing!

Bobby Deer from Quaqtaq, Nunavik, had been filming the meeting that night on his video camera from the back of the church sanctuary. When the Spirit of Generosity began to trigger the hearts of God's people, Bobby got off of the camera and quickly ran to the altar to empty out his entire wallet as he knew that God was working miracles! By the time Bobby got back to the video camera, he said that he could feel that his wallet had enlarged within his pant pocket. When he checked to see if money had supernaturally appeared, he was stunned to discover $1,500 miraculously placed inside his billfold! He began praising the Lord and thanking Him for His faithfulness!

"I will give you the treasures of darkness, riches stored in secret places, so that you may know that I am the LORD, the God of Israel, who summons you by name."
(Isaiah 45:3)

I don't understand exactly how this miracle happens. If I could figure it out in my natural mind, I guess it wouldn't be a real miracle. That is the "wonder" of what God is doing in the earth. He is releasing His possibilities into the midst of our impossibilities. Every time we have an opportunity to be generous, God is really giving us a divine appointment with blessing, favor and increase. Just as Isaiah prophesied, God wants to give you the "treasures of darkness, riches stored in secret places, so that you may know that I am the LORD."

The Holy Spirit knows where every lost treasure exists in the earth. He sees the hidden drug money, the forgotten inheritance stored behind walls and attic ceilings, the golden coins sunken in the depths of the sea, and I believe somehow He is able to transfer this wealth from one place to another. If God could supernaturally transport Philip (I mean a living, breathing human of flesh and bones) from one location to another (Acts 8:39-40), it shouldn't be difficult for us to believe that God can move paper money from the wicked to the righteous!

"...a sinner's wealth is stored up for the righteous."
(Proverbs 13:22)

Later that summer as we were ministering in Auckland, New Zealand, with Pastors David and Judy Collins, there was a wonderful night when financial miracles began taking place in the meeting. A realm opened up where people began to get out of their seats and got radical in their giving. Some people were led to go and sow seed into other people's lives, while others came and put their money into the offering buckets. As one Pastor went to give his last $50, another person was directed to go and sow a seed of $1000 into that Pastor's life! I mean, it was radical. People were really being led by the Spirit of God and also choosing to operate in a generous level of faith.

As the realm continued to build, I began to prophesy into the atmosphere and I declared that financial miracles were taking place in people's homes, ministries and bank accounts! I prophesied that God was going to supernaturally deposit money into somebody's bank account! This was a bold declaration, but the Scriptures tell us that God watches over His Word to perform it (Jeremiah 1:12). Sure enough, the next day we found out that two different ladies had received unexplainable bank account deposits. One received $38,000 and the other had received $41,000 from the Lord.

This was something new for us. This miracle has been a catalyst for the same thing to happen in countless other places, as we have shared this testimony in different cities around the world. Many other people have received supernatural bank account deposits and unexplainable blessings! *It's joy unspeakable and full of glory!*

As I was receiving an offering in Honolulu, Hawaii, at the Spiritual Hunger Conference with John and Linda Keough and Cal and Michele Pierce, there was a woman who felt led to give the very last of her money. It was like the widow's mite. She knew that she didn't have very much in her bank account but she wanted to give all that she had. As the offering was be-ing received, she called the bank to find out her balance so that she would be able to write a check without overdrawing her ac-count. As she spoke to the person on the phone, she found out that a large sum of money had been deposited into her account. These were funds that had been previously denied to her, but somehow, several thousands of dollars managed to be released into her bank account. These funds were enough to cover her son's tuition and to make her loudly rejoice with praise as she danced with her offering in hand! She had been praying for a breakthrough, and as she moved towards trusting God with her finances, it caused the miracle to come into her life! It was seedtime and harvest time at the same time!

> *"The days are coming," declares the LORD, "when the reaper will be overtaken by the plowman and the planter by the one treading grapes. New wine will drip from the mountains and flow from all the hills."* (Amos 9:13)

Miracles happen quickly in the glory because it is the realm of eternity. It is not limited to time and space (for more detailed teaching on this subject, you will find my book *Time & Eter-nity* filled with fascinating revelation). When you sow into the glory realm, you will begin to reap from that realm of unlimited potential. And you must understand that when the prosperity of God shows up in your life, it's not just financial blessings that begin to increase. You will observe miracles appearing in places you never dreamed possible. God desires to give you cre-ative solutions to your problems, and the answers for questions you've held in your mind for years.

The following testimony came to me from Pastor Kim in Seoul, Korea, after I had ministered in a series of meetings at the wonderful Yong Dong First Church:

> Ever since you left here, miracles are following those who attended the meeting. Miss Kwon who sat beside you at the buffet dinner table last Monday had a shocking supernatural touch of the Lord. She was working in her office when suddenly she heard her printer working. However, at the time she was not watching the printer. As she was going out, she passed the printer and saw the new design of the vest for this fall's fashion collection. She did not touch her computer and she checked with all her colleague's as to whether or not they sent one. Nobody did! She says that she wanted this same kind of vest design for this fall. She is very excited! After all, our Lord is the most creative designer! Even now we are eagerly waiting for your next visit. We are so thankful to the Lord that you came to Korea!

We don't always understand how God works, but we can always understand that He does work! His miracles are unending. As you participate with the realms of glory through your generosity, begin to expect for the Lord to give you creative ideas, new inventions, technologies and strategies that will lead you into realms of new success! As you're faithful to walk in this glory, you can expect the Lord to also give you wisdom concerning your debts.

Last year as I was ministering in Houston, Texas, a woman in the meeting was trusting God for a miracle breakthrough in her finances. That night she sowed a financial seed of $100 into the offering. She wrote back a few days later with a testimony that her $14,000 hospital bill had been completely forgiven! She received a miracle breakthrough of supernatural debt cancellation! In our ministry we have had a special anointing for these kinds of money miracles with thousands of testimonies from people who have received unusual blessings from God.

A single mother brought an offering to my meetings in Victoria, Canada, that became a source of supernatural supply for her family as she received two unexpected checks for $6,500 shortly after she had trusted God with her finances! She was able to pay the remaining balance for her son's college tuition and take care of her daughter's needs. God cares for you. This is why He has opened this realm of exponential increase for you.

Scatter Your Seed

As you scatter your seed into these divine appointments, you will begin to see that the Harvest Glory is surrounding your life. God desires to pour out His oil and His wine upon you! He wants to release His blessing, favor and increase through your life. The Bible says that the willing and obedient will eat the good of this land.

Are you willing? Are you ready to be obedient?

Next I'm going to take your revelation of these realms to a whole new level as we begin discovering the Angels of Prosperity that God has assigned over your life.

$\mathscr{R}$ELEASING ANGELS OF PROSPERITY

*Let them shout for joy and rejoice, who favor my
vindication; And let them say continually, "The
LORD be magnified, Who delights in the prosperity
of His servant." ~Psalm 35:27, NASB*

God wants to meet all of your needs according to His
riches in heavenly glory (Philippians 4:19). He desires
to fill your cup to overflowing so that you will be able to see a
need and be the vessel that God uses to release a miracle for
someone else!

Don't you want to be a miracle for someone else? I do!

When you begin moving in these realms of blessing, favor
and increase, suddenly you begin to realize that the possibilities
of God are unlimited and the provision in which we walk in is
unlimited too!

It's been said that God created His Angels to protect, direct and prosper His people. In this chapter I want to explore

the possibilities of God releasing His Angelic host into your life to cause you to prosper.

In my life I have had several encounters with Angels of Prosperity. I believe the Lord assigned these Angels to the first meetings where I began to receive a revelation about the power of sowing and reaping. God always assigns these particular Angels to release revelation about tithes, offerings and seed. These same Angels who bring this *revelation* of God's Word also deliver the *manifestation* of it.

Over a year and a half ago as I was resting in our Palm Springs rental home, after returning back from an overseas ministry trip to Asia, I had a dream where I saw an Angel of Prosperity come to me and he began to cover me with gold. I saw him releasing gold coins and finances along with gold dust and liquid gold splattering all over my hands and body, even overflowing from the pockets of my clothing!

We not only live among men, but there are airy hosts, blessed spectators, sympathetic lookers-on, that see and know and appreciate our thoughts and feelings and actions.
~Henry Ward Beecher

This dream was vivid in my mind when I awoke and came with an amazing realization that I was entering into a new dimension of prosperity and provision. At that moment Janet Angela came into our room and began to tell me that as she was folding our laundry, which had just come out of the washing machine and dryer, gold dust began appearing on my pants and then began overflowing from the pockets of our son's pants as well. When we began to relay this testimony by phone to our office assistant, Catherine, in Canada, she began to explain that at that very same time she began receiving gold dust on her forearms and all over her pants as well! We were experiencing a corporate visitation of the Angel of Prosperity!

I began to discern the realm, and I knew the first thing I needed to do was sow into this revelation. I have found that as I've sowed into the glory, as I can sense the tangible presence of the Lord, I have been able to reap a harvest of glory that produces greater results. So while the Spirit of God was moving and releasing these signs and wonders, and while the dream was still very vivid in my mind, I called a fellow minister and told them that I wanted to sow into their life. Just that day their air-conditioner had broken and I told them that I would pay for the entire $3,600 bill. This was my seed into what I was seeing the Lord do in our midst. I have learned to *respond* to the realm in order to *benefit* from the realm.

> *The evidence of God's presence, far outweighs the proof of His absence. ~Dr. Mike Murdock, Evangelist and Entrepreneur*

Just after I hung up the phone while I was getting changed to go to the airport, I reached into the pockets of my shorts and discovered that money had been put into my pockets! I'm not talking about just forgetting money in my shorts or some other natural explanation. I mean God had somehow placed paper bills into my pocket pants! This was enough to send me through the roof with excitement over the tremendous encounter we were experiencing!

When God sends an Angel of Prosperity to your home, get ready to be blessed beyond measure! In short, here are some of the amazing events that transpired in the following days after our Angelic encounter.

- We received an email from the Full Gospel Business Men's Fellowship in Singapore stating that more offerings had come in for our ministry even after we had left. They sent the money and it was a tremendous unexpected blessing!

- We received a new SUV vehicle we had been believing the Lord for over many years.

- After losing two employees, the Lord supernaturally increased our productivity and prospered the ministry in unprecedented ways!

- The Lord supernaturally enabled us to purchase two homes in one year, after renting apartments and leasing homes for eleven years of marriage! Now we have a home at both of our ministry base locations.

We have been living within this encounter and seeing God do some very amazing things!

> *"... The Lord, before whom I walk, will send His angel with you and prosper your way..."* (Genesis 24:40)

Do you realize that there are Angels of Prosperity that have been assigned over your life as well? Within the book of Hebrews, the Bible makes it clear that God created Angels to minister to the needs of Christians. In this book I have been sharing some biblical perspective and keys for unlocking the realms of blessing, favor and increase in your life. In financial matters, God desires to release these heavenly messengers to minister to your areas of lack, poverty and famine.

Even if you've never encountered a supernatural experience in your life, I want to open something up for you today that will change you forever! I believe that God is going to use this book to turn your situations around and that you're going to begin walking in these same things that I'm talking about as you're reading this book. In this chapter, I want to give you keys that will assist you in releasing these Angels of Prosperity over your life. You need to see these life-changing promises of God within His Word.

Their garments are white, but with an unearthly whiteness. These bright Angels are enveloped in a light so different from ours that by comparison everything else seems dark."
~Father Theodore Lamy, French Priest

Many Christians seem to be so down in the dumps regarding their finances because they haven't understood the promises within the Word of God pertaining to the realms of blessing, favor and increase. Hosea 4:6 says: *"My people are destroyed for lack of knowledge."* A limitation of *revelation* will bring a limitation of *manifestation*. We have seen this so many times within the Church, and it's such a sad thing because this is not the way it's supposed to be! God has called us to be those who walk according to His Word. I believe that as you've been reading this book the Lord has been

challenging you in regards to your finances and your heart atti-
tudes, because the revelation of God will always bring a breakthrough! Sometimes the biggest breakthrough you can receive
is from yourself!

> *For this reason we also, since the day we heard it, do
> not cease to pray for you, and to ask that you may be
> filled with the knowledge of His will in all wisdom
> and spiritual understanding; that you may walk
> worthy of the Lord, fully pleasing Him, being fruitful
> in every good work and increasing in the knowledge
> of God; strengthened with all might, according to His
> glorious power, for all patience and longsuffering with
> joy; giving thanks to the Father who has qualified us
> to be partakers of the inheritance of the saints in the
> light.* (Colossians 1:9-12)

Your natural mindset has limited your ability to perceive
the greatness of God's glory, but as the illumination of God's
revelation has been touching your spirit through this book, I
believe that something inside of you is beginning to stir and
you are receiving an impartation for prosperity! God has qualified you to be a partaker of this inheritance!

Don't allow your monthly budget to keep you back from
tithing. Don't permit your frequent bills to limit your giving,
and make sure you don't use your monthly rent or mortgage as
an excuse for not sowing seed. We need to allow the Holy Spirit to change our perspective on these things. We must even allow Him to change our vocabulary for money and our financial
resources. Instead of calling your monthly home loan a "mort-

gage," begin to call it a "home payment." Did you know that the word "mortgage" actually means "death-grip"! As a born again Bible believing Christian, the Lord hasn't assigned a death-grip on you. Quite to the contrary, Psalm 91:11-12 says, *"For He shall give His angels charge over you, to keep you in all your ways. In their hands they shall bear you up, lest you dash your foot against a stone."*

If you woo the company of the angels in your waking hours, they will be sure to come to you in your sleep. ~Anonymous

Words are so powerful (see Psalm 33:6; Hebrews 11:3; Matthew 12:36-37; Matthew 21:22). We must be careful not to speak curses over ourselves and our financial situation.

Right now I rebuke any word curse or spirit of lack that has tried to assign itself over your life. The Bible says that God has assigned his holy Angels to watch over your life! Oh praise the Lord with me! Hallelujah!

- The Lord has assigned His Angels to cover you with supernatural protection. (Psalm 91:11)
- The Lord has assigned His Angels to watch over your family. (Psalm 34:7)
- The Lord has assigned His Angels to minister health, healing and wholeness to your body. (John 5:4)
- The Lord has even assigned His Angels of Prosperity to begin moving in the midst of your financial well-being!

True prosperity is having enough to meet your own needs, with enough left over to meet the needs of others. This is why God is assigning these Angels to take charge over the affairs of your life as you walk in obedience to the Word of God.

As we walk in the ease of the glory realm, God assigns His Angels of Prosperity around us to ensure that our endeavors are blessed, favored, successful, and directed by Him.

> *"Behold, I send an Angel before you to keep you in the way and to bring you into the place which I have prepared."* (Exodus 23:20)

All throughout the Scriptures we see Angels of Prosperity at work in the lives of God's people, although they come in many forms. One of these Angels appeared to Elijah and baked him a cake and gave him this supernatural food to eat, which became strength for the journey ahead. This "Angel food" enabled Elijah to travel, strengthened in this miraculous way, for forty days and forty nights until he reached Mount Horeb.

> *...as he lay and slept under a broom tree, suddenly an angel touched him, and said to him, "Arise and eat." Then he looked, and there by his head was a cake baked on coals, and a jar of water. So he ate and drank, and lay down again. And the angel of the Lord came back the second time, and touched him, and said, "Arise and eat, because the journey is too great for you." So he arose, and ate and drank; and he went in the strength of that food forty days and forty nights as far as Horeb, the mountain of God.* (1 Kings 19:5-8)

Several years ago the Lord sent Janet and myself, along with a team, to the North Island of New Zealand to minister. We spent almost a month releasing the glory of God in numerous churches and locations. This was such an exciting adventure as we were experiencing the tangible presence of God in every single meeting! During this particular ministry trip the Lord began revealing the reality of the Angelic realm to us in a brand new way.

Angels descending, bring from above, echoes of mercy, whispers of love. ~Fanny J. Crosby, American Hymnist

In several meetings we were witnesses to the presence of Angels as beautiful white feathers began to flutter through the air and fall upon the people that were gathered in that atmosphere of the glory realm. One night we watched in amazement as the heavy curtains behind the pulpit began to sway back and forth as I was preaching about the reality of the unseen realm.

Even though the room was without air-conditioning vents and all the doors and windows were shut, some people still remained skeptical about this particular manifestation. Assuming that someone was pushing these curtains from behind, these skeptics went behind the curtains only to discover that what they were seeing was a genuine manifestation of the Angelic realm.

That night after the meeting many were down on their hands and knees picking up hundreds of tiny feathers from the floor. These small tokens of Angelic activity were again a testimony to the reality of God's heavenly messengers.

About half way through the month-long trip, some people on the team began feeling weary in their bodies because of the demanding travel and tight ministry schedule that we were maintaining. One night after our glorious meeting in Manakau, New Zealand, we returned to our hotel room only to find that the Angelic realm had been activated on our behalf to minister God's healing power to our physical bodies. The Lord sent an Angel, bringing us golden leaves from the trees in heaven. We were astonished as these delicate leaves had been placed so beautifully upon the open pages of the Holy Bible.

Angels can fly directly into the heart of the matter.
~Anonymous

In this state of awe, the Spirit of God began to give us instruction by revealing to one of the team members that these golden leaves were an edible source of strength, healing and supernatural empowerment. Just as Elijah had eaten the cake provided by Angels, we too began to partake of this heavenly substance as we ate these miraculous golden leaves that were wonderfully provided to give us strength.

Through this encounter we experienced the Lord releasing His Angels of Prosperity in our midst to bring wholeness to our bodies. The very next day, because of our new found strength, we journeyed by foot, along with our ministry team, on a round-trip trek to the top of Mount Rangitoto. This was so supernatural! We continued ministering for the rest of our

appointed schedule with a new found strength in the empowerment we received from the Lord. We rejoiced and thanked
Jesus Christ as He had allowed us to encounter His provision
in a brand new way. God chose to release this experience to us
through the remarkable ministry of Angels.

In the outstanding book *Angels On Assignment*, Pastor Ro-
land Buck shared a similar experience where the Angel Gabriel
appeared to him and instructed him to eat a small wafer and to
drink some water from a silver ladle. As Pastor Buck proceeded
to follow these Angelic instructions, his entire body was filled
with an overwhelming fizzing sensation, and over the course of
several days he began supernaturally losing weight!

> *Daniel answered, "May the king live forever! My
> God sent his angel, and he shut the mouths of the lions.
> They have not hurt me, because I was found innocent
> in his sight."* (Daniel 6:21)

Some ancient texts tell that when Daniel was trapped in
the Lion's den, a Prosperity Angel appeared to the Prophet
Habbakuk and instructed him to carry dinner to Daniel, in order for him to have something to eat during this time of great
trial. The Angel proceeded to lift Habbakuk through the air
and supernaturally placed him over the den.

In Genesis, Jacob saw Angels ascending and descending
upon a stairway between heaven and earth. I believe these Angels were releasing an impartation of prosperity and provision
to Jacob as they were drawing his attention to the Lord who
stood at the top, above this stairway. In this encounter, the Lord
promised to bless Jacob in the land where he would live.

The Lord stood above it and said: "I am the Lord God of Abraham your father and the God of Isaac; the land on which you lie I will give to you and your descendants. Also your descendants shall be as the dust of the earth; you shall spread abroad to the west and the east, to the north and the south; and in you and in your seed all the families of the earth shall be blessed. Behold, I am with you and will keep you wherever you go, and will bring you back to this land; for I will not leave you until I have done what I have spoken to you."(Genesis 28:13-15)

Wouldn't it be wonderful to wake up one morning and see these Angels with gifts of heavenly provision walking up and down the stairs in your home?! These encounters we read about in the Bible are available for you today because God has not changed His ways. As you're faithful to tithe, give offerings and plant seed into the work of God's kingdom, the Lord desires to touch your finances with His glory through the ministry of Prosperity Angels. Your obedience activates this realm of the open heavens!

The Bible makes it clear that even Abraham was accustomed to having these Prosperity Angels lead him as he traveled in the land of Canaan (Galatians 3:14 says that we can also receive the same blessings of Abraham). This was revealed when he sent his steward to look for a wife for his son Isaac, telling him that the Angel of the Lord would go before him.

"The Lord God of heaven, who took me from my father's house and from the land of my family, and who spoke

to me and swore to me, saying, 'To your descendants I give this land,' He will send His angel before you, and you shall take a wife for my son from there." (Genesis 24:7)

This Prosperity Angel did indeed lead the steward to the woman who would become Isaac's wife. The steward recounted his experience to Laban, and he told him that Abraham had prophesied that

I believe in Angels: Angels in heaven, on earth, and in the midmost air... guardian or tutelary angels steering our wayward course. ~Rose Macaulay, British Writer

"the Lord, before whom I walk, will send His angel with you and prosper your way; and you shall take a wife for my son from my family and from my father's house" (Genesis 24:40). Through this passage of Scripture, we discover that the successful choice of a mate is even considered to be a sign of prosperity!

If you're currently single and in need of a husband or wife, I believe that God has the perfect match for you. God wants to give you His best! Right now you can begin releasing these Prosperity Angels to go ahead of you and prosper your way! These Prosperity Angels are assigned from heaven to prepare the way before you. God has assigned them as ministering spirits to your life in order that you would be led into the realms of blessing, favor and increase with great success, abundance and outstanding opportunities!

Yes, that's right, I said that God has made provision for His Angels of Prosperity to move on your behalf in regards to your every need!

An Angel of Prosperity spoke to Jacob in a dream and gave him a revelation for success. The Angel told Jacob how to mate specific animals that would be strong and reproduce in great abundance.

"And it happened, at the time when the flocks conceived, that I lifted my eyes and saw in a dream, and behold, the rams which leaped upon the flocks were streaked, speckled, and gray-spotted. Then the Angel of God spoke to me in a dream, saying, 'Jacob.' And I said, 'Here I am.' And He said, 'Lift your eyes now and see, all the rams which leap on the flocks are streaked, speckled, and gray-spotted; for I have seen all that Laban is doing to you. I am the God of Bethel, where you anointed the pillar and where you made a vow to Me. Now arise, get out of this land, and return to the land of your family.'" (Genesis 31:10-13)

I believe that God desires to release His Prosperity Angels to speak holy revelations of wisdom from heaven into your life, even through your dreams. God desires to give you witty ideas and creative ideas that will lead you into great success.

I wisdom dwell with prudence, and find out knowledge of witty inventions. (Proverbs 8:12, KJV)

The book of Psalms speaks about a poor man who was rescued from his troubles of poverty through the deliverance ministry of an Angel of Prosperity.

This poor man cried out, and the Lord heard him, and saved him out of all his troubles. The angel of the Lord encamps all around those who fear Him, and delivers them. (Psalm 34:6-7)

Believers, look up - take courage. The angels are nearer than you think. ~Billy Graham, American Evangelist

In Luke 22:43 we discover that even Jesus Christ during his time here on earth received the ministry of Angels as a strengthening and empowerment for His journey to the cross of Calvary. I believe that God wants to unlock the realms of blessing, favor and increase in your life through the ministry work of His Angels of Prosperity as you are obedient to follow God's instructions through His Word.

As I've already shared, your tithe, offerings and seed are first and foremost in activating these realms of blessing, favor and increase. We see that Cornelius understood this, as Acts 10 shows us the connection between his financial giving and the visitation of an Angel in his home. Let's look at three areas of obedience to God that will bring immeasurable benefits to your life!

3 AREAS OF OBEDIENCE THAT CAUSE PROSPERITY ANGELS TO RESPOND TO YOUR NEED

1.   OBEDIENCE TO BELIEVE THE WORD

You must believe the Word of God. What does God's Word say about your prosperity? Do you believe that God wants to bless your life with overflowing abundance and the true riches of His glory? Obedience to believe God's Word will cause you to receive the blessings from it.

> *"You will be blessed in the city and blessed in the country. The fruit of your womb will be blessed, and the crops of your land and the young of your livestock— the calves of your herds and the lambs of your flocks. Your basket and your kneading trough will be blessed. You will be blessed when you come in and blessed when you go out. The Lord will grant that the enemies who rise up against you will be defeated before you. They will come at you from one direction but flee from you in seven. The Lord will send a blessing on your barns and on everything you put your hand to. The Lord your God will bless you in the land he is giving you. The Lord will establish you as his holy people, as he promised you on oath, if you keep the commands of the Lord your God and walk in his ways. Then all the peoples on earth will see that you are called by the name of the Lord, and they will fear you. The Lord will grant you abundant prosperity."* (Deuteronomy 28:3-10)

2.   OBEDIENCE TO SPEAK THE WORD

What do you want to produce in your life? I mentioned earlier that your words are powerful. The Bible gives us some clear advice about the words that we choose to speak. *"Death and life are in the power of the tongue, and those who love it will eat its fruit"* (Proverbs 18:21). Your words contain the ability to breathe life on situations and circumstances that surround you. As you've now purposed in your heart to diligently pursue a life of blessing, favor and increase, I want you to begin changing the way that you speak about your finances. The best thing that you can do is declare the Word of God over your money, over your bills and over your household. Begin speaking life into areas that look so hopeless in the natural. Negative and doubt-filled words will keep your Angels bound and unable to produce positive results. But words filled with faith will release them into working victories for you! The Scriptures give us understanding that your words are one of the keys to releasing Angels of Prosperity in your life!

T he guardian Angels of life fly so high as to be beyond our sight, but they are always looking down upon us.
~Johann Paul Richter

> **Bless the Lord, you His angels, who excel in strength, who do His word, heeding the voice of His word.** (Psalm 103:20)

Wow! Did you see that? The Angels of God are exhorted to bless the Lord by doing His word. The Bible says that they heed unto the voice of His Word. In other words, you need to speak the Word, and when you speak the Word, it gives "voice" to God's will and puts the Angels of God to work! Negative and doubt-filled words will give opportunity for demonic spirits to act, but faith-filled and positive words will encourage the heavenly Angelic realm to work on your behalf! I believe many times we have not seen the results that we've desired because we haven't given our Angels any jobs to do. Speaking words of doubt and unbelief over your finances will not release Prosperity Angels into your situation. These Angels are waiting to hear the voice of God's Word! They are waiting to hear the voice of faith! Begin speaking God's Word over your finances right now. As you do, believe that God is watching over His Word to perform it by appointing Angels of Prosperity to your declarations!

> *Millions of spiritual creatures walk the earth unseen, both when we wake and when we sleep. ~John Milton, English Poet*

3. OBEDIENCE TO DO THE WORD

As you begin *believing* the Word, *speaking* the Word, and you begin *doing* the Word, the results will be phenomenal! The Scriptures clearly tell us to **"be doers of the word, and not hearers only"** (James 1:22), and **"faith without works is dead"** (James 2:20). When you begin putting the principles of this book into action, you are going to begin seeing a change in your situations. Faith always takes action. Purpose to be more faithful in the stewardship of your finances, and begin purposing to walk-out this revelation through paying your tithes, giving offerings and sowing seed into fertile soil (ministries that are producing good results!). Faith is the PIN code that will open your account at God's ATM!

God does want to meet all of your needs and His riches in heavenly glory are more than enough! This includes Angels who perform His word to fill your cup to overflowing so that you will be able to bless those around you. Receive all that God has for you and be a miracle for someone else!

The possibilities of God are unlimited and the provision in which we walk in is unlimited too!

CHAPTER EIGHT

*P*OSITION YOURSELF FOR PROSPERITY!

The very first step to position yourself for prosperity is to have a personal relationship with Jesus Christ. Do you know Him? The Bible says:

> *That if you confess with your mouth, "Jesus is Lord," and believe in your heart that God raised him from the dead, you will be saved. For it is with your heart that you believe and are justified, and it is with your mouth that you confess and are saved.* Romans 10:9-10

If you want to give your life to Christ, pray this with me:

> *Father, thank you for forgiving my sins. Jesus, come into my heart. Make me the kind of person You want me to be. Thank you for saving me. Amen.*

The Bible is very clear that *"everyone who calls on the name of the Lord will be saved"* (Romans 10:13). Welcome to the family of God! Please use the contact information on the Resources page after Chapter 12 to let us know that you have chosen to follow Christ, and we will send you a free gift called "Starting Your New Life" (Item #IT-01) to help you grow strong in your new relationship with Christ.

Confess, Obey, Accelerate!

The next four chapters contain Scriptures that you can begin activating and declaring over your life. These powerful confessions, along with your obedience to do the Word, are guaranteed to accelerate you into experiencing the greatest wave of abundance you've ever known.

Remember:

- **There is a blessing on the other side of every tithe.**
- **There is financial favor on the other side of every offering.**
- **There is an intended harvest on the other side of every seed.**

The key is that they must all be released into the glory in order for you to experience the miracle at the other side! God will always ask you to do something possible so that He can do something impossible. Will you trust God with all He has entrusted to you? *Yes*

Throughout your life, God desires to unlock the realms of blessing, favor and increase! Are you ready to receive these realms? Are you ready to unlock these dimensions of unlimited potential with Angels of prosperity?

The truths I've shared with you in this book, when applied, will cause you to be **Positioned For Prosperity**.

CHAPTER NINE

*P*ROSPERITY ANGEL SCRIPTURES

Genesis 24:40

"He replied, 'The LORD, before whom I have walked faithfully, will send his angel with you and make your journey a success, so that you can get a wife for my son from my own clan and from my father's family.'" Tribe ☺

Genesis 48:15-16

Then he blessed Joseph and said, "May the God before whom my fathers Abraham and Isaac walked faithfully, the God who has been my shepherd all my life to this day, the Angel who has delivered me from all harm may he bless these boys. May they be called by my name and the names of my fathers Abraham and Isaac, and may they increase greatly upon the earth."

Exodus 23:20-30

"See, I am sending an angel ahead of you to guard you along the way and to bring you to the place I have prepared. Pay attention to him and listen to what he says. Do not rebel against him; he will not forgive your rebellion, since my Name is in him. If you listen carefully to what he says and do all that I say, I will be an enemy to your enemies and will oppose those who oppose you. My angel will go ahead of you and bring you into the land of the Amorites, Hittites, Perizzites, Canaanites, Hivites and Jebusites, and I will wipe them out. Do not bow down before their gods or worship them or follow their practices. You must demolish them and break their sacred stones to pieces. Worship the LORD your God, and his blessing will be on your food and water. I will take away sickness from among you, and none will miscarry or be barren in your land. I will give you a full life span.

"I will send my terror ahead of you and throw into confusion every nation you encounter. I will make all your enemies turn their backs and run. I will send the hornet ahead of you to drive the Hivites, Canaanites and Hittites out of your way. But I will not drive them out in a single year, because the land would become desolate and the wild animals too numerous for you. Little by little I will drive them out before you, until you have increased enough to take possession of the land."

Psalm 34:6-10

This poor man called, and the LORD heard him; he saved him out of all his troubles. The angel of the LORD encamps around those who fear him, and he delivers them.

Taste and see that the LORD is good; blessed is the one who takes refuge in him. Fear the LORD, you his holy people, for those who fear him lack nothing. The lions may grow weak and hungry, but those who seek the LORD lack no good thing.

Psalm 91:11

For he will command his angels concerning you to guard you in all your ways.

Psalm 103:19-22

The LORD has established his throne in heaven, and his kingdom rules over all. Praise the LORD, you his angels, you mighty ones who do his bidding, who obey his word. Praise the LORD, all his heavenly hosts, you his servants who do his will. Praise the LORD, all his works everywhere in his dominion. Praise the LORD, my soul.

Ecclesiastes 5:4-6

When you make a vow to God, do not delay to fulfill it. He has no pleasure in fools; fulfill your vow. It is better not to make a vow than to make one and not fulfill it. Do not let your mouth lead you into sin. And do not protest to the temple messenger, "My vow was a mistake." Why should God be angry at what you say and destroy the work of your hands?

Luke 6:27-38

"But to you who are listening I say: Love your enemies, do good to those who hate you, bless those who curse you, pray for those who mistreat you. If someone slaps you on one cheek, turn to them the other also. If someone takes your coat, do not withhold your shirt from them. Give to everyone who asks you, and if anyone takes what belongs to you, do not demand it back. Do to others as you would have them do to you.

"If you love those who love you, what credit is that to you? Even sinners love those who love them. And if you do good to those who are good to you, what credit is that to you? Even sinners do that. And if you lend to those from whom you expect repayment, what credit is that to you? Even sinners lend to sinners, expecting to be repaid in full. But love your enemies, do good to them, and lend to them without expecting to get anything back. Then your reward will be great, and you will be children of the Most High, because he is kind to the ungrateful and wicked. Be merciful, just as your Father is merciful.

"Do not judge, and you will not be judged. Do not condemn, and you will not be condemned. Forgive, and you will be forgiven. Give, and it will be given to you. A good measure, pressed down, shaken together and running over, will be poured into your lap. For with the measure you use, it will be measured to you."

Luke 15:17-24

"When he came to his senses, he said, 'How many of my father's hired servants have food to spare, and here I am starving to death! I will set out and go back to my father and say to him: Father, I have sinned against heaven and against you. I am no longer worthy to be called your son; make me like one of your hired servants.' So he got up and went to his father.

"But while he was still a long way off, his father saw him and was filled with compassion for him; he ran to his son, threw his arms around him and kissed him.

"The son said to him, 'Father, I have sinned against heaven and against you. I am no longer worthy to be called your son.'

"But the father said to his servants, 'Quick! Bring the best robe and put it on him. Put a ring on his finger and sandals on his feet. Bring the fattened calf and kill it. Let's have a feast and celebrate. For this son of mine was dead and is alive again; he was lost and is found.' So they began to celebrate."

1 Corinthians 9:9-11

For it is written in the Law of Moses: "Do not muzzle an ox while it is treading out the grain." Is it about oxen that God is concerned? Surely he says this for us, doesn't he? Yes, this was written for us, because whoever plows and threshes should be able to do so in the hope of sharing in the harvest. If we have sown spiritual seed among you, is it too much if we reap a material harvest from you?

Hebrews 1:13-14

To which of the angels did God ever say, "Sit at my right hand until I make your enemies a footstool for your feet"? Are not all angels ministering spirits sent to serve those who will inherit salvation?

$\mathscr{S}$CRIPTURE KEYS FOR BLESSING

OLD TESTAMENT

Genesis 12:1-3

The LORD had said to Abram, "Go from your country, your people and your father's household to the land I will show you. "I will make you into a great nation and I will bless you; I will make your name great, and you will be a blessing. I will bless those who bless you, and whoever curses you I will curse; and all peoples on earth will be blessed through you."

Genesis 13 :2

Abram had become very wealthy in livestock and in silver and gold.

Genesis 15:1

After this, the word of the LORD came to Abram in a vision: "Do not be afraid, Abram. I am your shield, your very great reward."

Genesis 24:34, 35

So he said, "I am Abraham's servant. The LORD has blessed my master abundantly, and he has become wealthy. He has given him sheep and cattle, silver and gold, male and female servants, and camels and donkeys.

Genesis 24:40

"He replied, 'The LORD, before whom I have walked faithfully, will send his angel with you and make your journey a success, so that you can get a wife for my son from my own clan and from my father's family."

Genesis 26:2-5

The LORD appeared to Isaac and said, "Do not go down to Egypt; live in the land where I tell you to live. Stay in this land for a while, and I will be with you and will bless you. For to you and your descendants I will give all these lands and will confirm the oath I swore to your father Abraham. I will make your descendants as numerous as the stars in the sky and will give them all these lands, and through your offspring all nations on earth will be blessed, because Abraham obeyed me and did everything I required of him, keeping my commands, my decrees and my instructions."

Genesis 27:28, 29

"May God give you heaven's dew and earth's richness—an abundance of grain and new wine. May nations serve you and peoples bow down to you. Be lord over your brothers, and may the sons of your mother bow down to you. May those who curse you be cursed and those who bless you be blessed."

Genesis 28:3, 4

"May God Almighty bless you and make you fruitful and increase your numbers until you become a community of peoples. May he give you and your descendants the blessing given to Abraham, so that you may take possession of the land where you now reside as a foreigner, the land God gave to Abraham."

Genesis 28:20-22

Then Jacob made a vow, saying, "If God will be with me and will watch over me on this journey I am taking and will give me food to eat and clothes to wear so that I return safely to my father's household, then the LORD will be my God and this stone that I have set up as a pillar will be God's house, and of all that you give me I will give you a tenth."

Genesis 30:27-30

But Laban said to him, "If I have found favor in your eyes, please stay. I have learned by divination that the LORD has blessed me because of you." He added, "Name your wages, and I will pay them." Jacob said to him, "You know how I have worked for you and how your livestock has fared under my care. The little you had before I came has increased greatly, and the LORD has blessed you wherever I have been. But now, when may I do something for my own household?"

Genesis 48:15, 16

Then he blessed Joseph and said, "May the God before whom my fathers Abraham and Isaac walked faithfully, the God who has been my shepherd all my life to this day, the

Angel who has delivered me from all harm—may he bless these boys. May they be called by my name and the names of my fathers Abraham and Isaac, and may they increase greatly on the earth."

Genesis 49:22-26

"Joseph is a fruitful vine, a fruitful vine near a spring, whose branches climb over a wall.

With bitterness archers attacked him; they shot at him with hostility. But his bow remained steady, his strong arms stayed limber, because of the hand of the Mighty One of Jacob, because of the Shepherd, the Rock of Israel, because of your father's God, who helps you, because of the Almighty, who blesses you with blessings of the skies above, blessings of the deep springs below, blessings of the breast and womb. Your father's blessings are greater than the blessings of the ancient mountains, than the bounty of the age-old hills. Let all these rest on the head of Joseph, on the brow of the prince among his brothers.

Leviticus 23:10

"Speak to the Israelites and say to them: 'When you enter the land I am going to give you and you reap its harvest, bring to the priest a sheaf of the first grain you harvest.

Leviticus 27:30

"A tithe of everything from the land, whether grain from the soil or fruit from the trees, belongs to the LORD; it is holy to the LORD.

Numbers 6:22-27

The LORD said to Moses, "Tell Aaron and his sons, 'This is how you are to bless the Israelites. Say to them: ""'The LORD bless you and keep you; the LORD make his face shine on you and be gracious to you; the LORD turn his face toward you and give you peace.'" "So they will put my name on the Israelites, and I will bless them."

Numbers 22:12

But God said to Balaam, "Do not go with them. You must not put a curse on those people, because they are blessed."

Numbers 23:19, 20

God is not human, that he should lie, not a human being, that he should change his mind.

Does he speak and then not act? Does he promise and not fulfill? I have received a command to bless; he has blessed, and I cannot change it.

Deuteronomy 2:7

The LORD your God has blessed you in all the work of your hands. He has watched over your journey through this vast wilderness. These forty years the LORD your God has been with you, and you have not lacked anything.

Deuteronomy 8:10-18

When you have eaten and are satisfied, praise the LORD your God for the good land he has given you. Be careful that you do not forget the LORD your God, failing to observe his commands, his laws and his decrees that I am giving you this day. Otherwise, when you eat and are satisfied, when you build fine houses and settle down, and when your herds and flocks grow large and your silver and gold increase and all you have is multiplied, then your heart will become proud and you will forget the LORD your God, who brought you out of Egypt, out of the land of slavery. He led you through the vast and dreadful wilderness, that thirsty and waterless land, with its venomous snakes and scorpions. He brought you water out of hard rock. He gave you manna to eat in the wilderness, something your ancestors had never known, to humble and test you so that in the end it might go well with you. You may say to yourself, "My power and the strength of my hands have produced this wealth for me." But remember the LORD your God, for it is he who gives you the ability to produce wealth, and so confirms his covenant, which he swore to your ancestors, as it is today.

Deuteronomy 14:22-29

Be sure to set aside a tenth of all that your fields produce each year. Eat the tithe of your grain, new wine and olive oil, and the firstborn of your herds and flocks in the presence of the LORD your God at the place he will choose as a dwelling for his Name, so that you may learn to revere the LORD your God always. But if that place is too distant and you have been blessed by the LORD your God and cannot carry your tithe (because the place where the LORD will choose to put his Name is so far away), then exchange your tithe for silver, and take the silver with you and go to the place the LORD your God will choose. Use the silver to buy whatever you like: cattle, sheep, wine or other fermented drink, or anything you wish. Then you and your household shall eat there in the presence of the LORD your God and rejoice. And do not neglect the Levites living in your towns, for they have no allotment or inheritance of their own. At the end of every three years, bring all the tithes of that year's produce and store it in your towns, so that the Levites (who have no allotment or inheritance of their own) and the foreigners, the fatherless and the widows who live in your towns may come and eat and be satisfied, and so that the LORD your God may bless you in all the work of your hands.

Deuteronomy 15:4-6

However, there need be no poor people among you, for in the land the LORD your God is giving you to possess as your inheritance, he will richly bless you, if only you fully obey the LORD your God and are careful to follow all these commands I am giving you today. For the LORD your God will bless you as he has promised, and you will lend to many nations but will borrow from none. You will rule over many nations but none will rule over you.

Deuteronomy 18:4, 5

You are to give them the firstfruits of your grain, new wine and olive oil, and the first wool from the shearing of your sheep, for the LORD your God has chosen them and their descendants out of all your tribes to stand and minister in the LORD's name always.

Deuteronomy 23:5

However, the LORD your God would not listen to Balaam but turned the curse into a blessing for you, because the LORD your God loves you.

Deuteronomy 23:19, 20

Do not charge a fellow Israelite interest, whether on money or food or anything else that may earn interest. You may charge a foreigner interest, but not a fellow Israelite, so that the LORD your God may bless you in everything you put your hand to in the land you are entering to possess.

Deuteronomy 24:19-22

When you are harvesting in your field and you overlook a sheaf, do not go back to get it. Leave it for the foreigner, the fatherless and the widow, so that the LORD your God may bless you in all the work of your hands. When you beat the olives from your trees, do not go over the branches a second time. Leave what remains for the foreigner, the fatherless and the widow. When you harvest the grapes in your vineyard, do not go over the vines again. Leave what remains for the foreigner, the fatherless and the widow. Remember that you were slaves in Egypt. That is why I command you to do this.

Deuteronomy 28:1-13

If you fully obey the LORD your God and carefully follow all his commands I give you today, the LORD your God will set you high above all the nations on earth. All these blessings will come on you and accompany you if you obey the LORD your God: You will be blessed in the city and blessed in the country. The fruit of your womb will be blessed, and the crops of your land and the young of your livestock—the calves of your herds and the lambs of your flocks. Your basket and your kneading trough will be blessed. You will be blessed when you come in and blessed when you go out. The LORD will grant that the enemies who rise up against you will be defeated before you. They will come at you from one direction but flee from you in seven. The LORD will send a blessing on your barns and on everything you put your hand to. The LORD your God will bless you in the land he is giving you. The LORD will establish you as his holy people, as he promised you on oath, if you keep the commands of the LORD your God and walk in obedience to him. Then all the peoples on earth will see that you are called by the name of the LORD, and they will fear you. The LORD will grant you abundant prosperity—in the fruit of your womb, the young of your livestock and the crops of your ground—in the land he swore to your ancestors to give you. The LORD will open the heavens, the storehouse of his bounty, to send rain on your land in season and to bless all the work of your hands. You will lend to many nations but will borrow from none. The LORD will make you the head, not the tail. If you pay attention to the commands of the LORD your God that I give you this day and carefully follow them, you will always be at the top, never at the bottom.

Deuteronomy 29:9

Carefully follow the terms of this covenant, so that you may prosper in everything you do.

Deuteronomy 30:19

This day I call the heavens and the earth as witnesses against you that I have set before you life and death, blessings and curses. Now choose life, so that you and your children may live

Deuteronomy 33:11

Bless all his skills, LORD, and be pleased with the work of his hands. Strike down those who rise against him, his foes till they rise no more."

Joshua 1:7-9

"Be strong and very courageous. Be careful to obey all the law my servant Moses gave you; do not turn from it to the right or to the left, that you may be successful wherever you go. Keep this Book of the Law always on your lips; meditate on it day and night, so that you may be careful to do every-thing written in it. Then you will be prosperous and success-ful. Have I not commanded you? Be strong and courageous. Do not be afraid; do not be discouraged, for the LORD your God will be with you wherever you go."

Ruth 2:12

May the LORD repay you for what you have done. May you be richly rewarded by the LORD, the God of Israel, under whose wings you have come to take refuge."

2 Samuel 6:11, 12

The ark of the LORD remained in the house of Obed-Edom the Gittite for three months, and the LORD blessed him and his entire household. Now King David was told, "The LORD has blessed the household of Obed-Edom and everything he has, because of the ark of God." So David went to bring up the ark of God from the house of Obed-Edom to the City of David with rejoicing.

2 Samuel 7:28, 29

Sovereign LORD, you are God! Your covenant is trustworthy, and you have promised these good things to your servant. Now be pleased to bless the house of your servant, that it may continue forever in your sight; for you, Sovereign LORD, have spoken, and with your blessing the house of your servant will be blessed forever."

1 Kings 2:2, 3

"I am about to go the way of all the earth," he said. "So be strong, act like a man, and observe what the LORD your God requires: Walk in obedience to him, and keep his decrees and commands, his laws and regulations, as written in the Law of Moses. Do this so that you may prosper in all you do and wherever you go

1 Chronicles 4:9, 10

Jabez was more honorable than his brothers. His mother had named him Jabez, saying, "I gave birth to him in pain." Jabez cried out to the God of Israel, "Oh, that you would bless me and enlarge my territory! Let your hand be with me, and keep me from harm so that I will be free from pain." And God granted his request.

1 Chronicles 17:23-27

"And now, LORD, let the promise you have made concerning your servant and his house be established forever. Do as you promised, so that it will be established and that your name will be great forever. Then people will say, 'The LORD Almighty, the God over Israel, is Israel's God!' And the house of your servant David will be established before you. "You, my God, have revealed to your servant that you will build a house for him. So your servant has found courage to pray to you. You, LORD, are God! You have promised these good things to your servant. Now you have been pleased to bless the house of your servant, that it may continue forever in your sight; for you, LORD, have blessed it, and it will be blessed forever."

1 Chronicles 22:11-13

"Now, my son, the LORD be with you, and may you have success and build the house of the LORD your God, as he said you would. May the LORD give you discretion and understanding when he puts you in command over Israel, so that you may keep the law of the LORD your God. Then you will have success if you are careful to observe the decrees and laws that the LORD gave Moses for Israel. Be strong and courageous. Do not be afraid or discouraged.

1 Chronicles 29:28

He died at a good old age, having enjoyed long life, wealth and honor. His son Solomon succeeded him as king.

2 Chronicles 31:6-10

The people of Israel and Judah who lived in the towns of Judah also brought a tithe of their herds and flocks and a tithe of the holy things dedicated to the LORD their God, and they piled them in heaps. They began doing this in the third month and finished in the seventh month. When Hezekiah and his officials came and saw the heaps, they praised the LORD and blessed his people Israel. Hezekiah asked the priests and Levites about the heaps; and Azariah the chief priest, from the family of Zadok, answered, "Since the people began to bring their contributions to the temple of the LORD, we have had enough to eat and plenty to spare, because the LORD has blessed his people, and this great amount is left over."

2 Chronicles 31:20, 21

This is what Hezekiah did throughout Judah, doing what was good and right and faithful before the LORD his God. In everything that he undertook in the service of God's temple and in obedience to the law and the commands, he sought his God and worked wholeheartedly. And so he prospered.

Psalm 1:1-3

Blessed is the one who does not walk in step with the wicked or stand in the way that sinners take or sit in the company of mockers, but whose delight is in the law of the LORD, and who meditates on his law day and night. That person is like a tree planted by streams of water, which yields its fruit in season and whose leaf does not wither— whatever they do prospers.

Psalm 3:1-8

LORD, how many are my foes! How many rise up against me! Many are saying of me, "God will not deliver him." But you, LORD, are a shield around me, my glory, the One who lifts my head high. I call out to the LORD, and he answers me from his holy mountain. I lie down and sleep; I wake again, because the LORD sustains me. I will not fear though tens of thousands assail me on every side. Arise, LORD! Deliver me, my God! Strike all my enemies on the jaw; break the teeth of the wicked. From the LORD comes deliverance. May your blessing be on your people.

Psalm 5:11, 12

But let all who take refuge in you be glad; let them ever sing for joy. Spread your protection over them, that those who love your name may rejoice in you. Surely, LORD, you bless the righteous; you surround them with your favor as with a shield.

Psalm 34:4-10

I sought the LORD, and he answered me; he delivered me from all my fears. Those who look to him are radiant; their faces are never covered with shame. This poor man called, and the LORD heard him; he saved him out of all his troubles. The angel of the LORD encamps around those who fear him, and he delivers them. Taste and see that the LORD is good; blessed is the one who takes refuge in him. Fear the LORD, you his holy people, for those who fear him lack nothing. The lions may grow weak and hungry, but those who seek the LORD lack no good thing.

Psalm 35:27

May those who delight in my vindication shout for joy and gladness; may they always say, "The LORD be exalted, who delights in the well-being of his servant."

Psalm 37:1-6

Do not fret because of those who are evil or be envious of those who do wrong; for like the grass they will soon wither, like green plants they will soon die away. Trust in the LORD and do good; dwell in the land and enjoy safe pasture. Take delight in the LORD, and he will give you the desires of your heart. Commit your way to the LORD; trust in him and he will do this: He will make your righteous reward shine like the dawn, your vindication like the noonday sun.

Psalm 41:1, 2

Blessed are those who have regard for the weak; the LORD delivers them in times of trouble. The LORD protects and preserves them—they are counted among the blessed in the land—he does not give them over to the desire of their foes.

Psalm 62:5-12

Yes, my soul, find rest in God; my hope comes from him. Truly he is my rock and my salvation; he is my fortress, I will not be shaken. My salvation and my honor depend on God; he is my mighty rock, my refuge. Trust in him at all times, you people; pour out your hearts to him, for God is our refuge. Surely the lowborn are but a breath, the highborn are but a lie. If weighed on a balance, they are nothing; together they are only a breath. Do not trust in extortion or put vain hope in stolen goods; though your riches increase, do not set your heart on them. One thing God has spoken, two things I have heard: "Power belongs to you, God, and with you, Lord, is unfailing love"; and, "You reward everyone according to what they have done."

Psalm 65:4

Blessed are those you choose and bring near to live in your courts! We are filled with the good things of your house, of your holy temple.

Psalm 68:17-20

The chariots of God are tens of thousands and thousands of thousands; the Lord has come from Sinai into his sanctuary. When you ascended on high, you took many captives; you received gifts from people, even from the rebellious— that you, LORD God, might dwell there. Praise be to the Lord, to God our Savior, who daily bears our burdens. Our God is a God who saves; from the Sovereign LORD comes escape from death.

Psalm 78:18-29

They willfully put God to the test by demanding the food they craved. They spoke against God; they said, "Can God really spread a table in the wilderness? True, he struck the rock, and water gushed out, streams flowed abundantly, but can he also give us bread? Can he supply meat for his people?" When the LORD heard them, he was furious; his fire broke out against Jacob, and his wrath rose against Israel, for they did not believe in God or trust in his deliverance. Yet he gave a command to the skies above and opened the doors of the heavens; he rained down manna for the people to eat, he gave them the grain of heaven. Human beings ate the bread of angels; he sent them all the food they could eat. He let loose the east wind from the heavens and by his power made the south wind blow. He rained meat down on them like dust, birds like sand on the seashore. He made them come down inside their camp, all around their tents. They ate till they were gorged—he had given them what they craved.

Psalm 84:4-12

Blessed are those who dwell in your house; they are ever praising you. Blessed are those whose strength is in you, whose hearts are set on pilgrimage. As they pass through the Valley of Baka, they make it a place of springs; the autumn rains also cover it with pools. They go from strength to strength, till each appears before God in Zion. Hear my prayer, LORD God Almighty; listen to me, God of Jacob. Look on our shield, O God; look with favor on your anointed one. Better is one day in your courts than a thousand elsewhere; I would rather be a doorkeeper in the house of my God than dwell in the tents of the wicked. For the LORD God is a sun and shield; the LORD bestows favor and honor; no good thing does he withhold from those whose walk is blameless. LORD Almighty, blessed is the one who trusts in you.

Psalm 112:1

Praise the LORD. Blessed are those who fear the LORD, who find great delight in his commands.

Psalm 115:11-13

You who fear him, trust in the LORD—he is their help and shield. The LORD remembers us and will bless us: He will bless his people Israel, he will bless the house of Aaron, he will bless those who fear the LORD—small and great alike.

Psalm 128:1-4

Blessed are all who fear the LORD, who walk in obedience to him. You will eat the fruit of your labor; blessings and prosperity will be yours. Your wife will be like a fruitful vine within your house; your children will be like olive shoots around your table. Yes, this will be the blessing for the man who fears the LORD.

Psalm 147:10-15

His pleasure is not in the strength of the horse, nor his delight in the legs of the warrior; the LORD delights in those who fear him, who put their hope in his unfailing love. Extol the LORD, Jerusalem; praise your God, Zion. He strengthens the bars of your gates and blesses your people within you. He grants peace to your borders and satisfies you with the finest of wheat. He sends his command to the earth; his word runs swiftly.

Proverbs 3:9-10

Honor the LORD with your wealth, with the firstfruits of all your crops; then your barns will be filled to overflowing, and your vats will brim over with new wine.

Proverbs 3:13-17

Blessed are those who find wisdom, those who gain understanding, for she is more profitable than silver and yields better returns than gold. She is more precious than rubies; nothing you desire can compare with her. Long life is in her right hand; in her left hand are riches and honor. Her ways are pleasant ways, and all her paths are peace.

Proverbs 8:32-34

"Now then, my children, listen to me; blessed are those who keep my ways. Listen to my instruction and be wise; do not disregard it. Blessed are those who listen to me, watching daily at my doors, waiting at my doorway.

Proverbs 10:22

The blessing of the LORD brings wealth, without painful toil for it.

Proverbs 11:11

Through the blessing of the upright a city is exalted, but by the mouth of the wicked it is destroyed.

Proverbs 11:16

A kindhearted woman gains honor, but ruthless men gain only wealth.

Proverbs 28:13

Whoever conceals their sins does not prosper, but the one who confesses and renounces them finds mercy.

Proverbs 28:20

A faithful person will be richly blessed, but one eager to get rich will not go unpunished.

Ecclesiastes 5:4

When you make a vow to God, do not delay to fulfill it. He has no pleasure in fools; fulfill your vow.

Isaiah 1:19, 20

If you are willing and obedient, you will eat the good things of the land; but if you resist and rebel, you will be devoured by the sword." For the mouth of the LORD has spoken.

Isaiah 32:17-20

The fruit of that righteousness will be peace; its effect will be quietness and confidence forever. My people will live in peaceful dwelling places, in secure homes, in undisturbed places of rest. Though hail flattens the forest and the city is leveled completely, how blessed you will be, sowing your seed by every stream, and letting your cattle and donkeys range free.

Isaiah 51:2, 3

look to Abraham, your father, and to Sarah, who gave you birth. When I called him he was only one man, and I blessed him and made him many. The LORD will surely comfort Zion and will look with compassion on all her ruins; he will make her deserts like Eden, her wastelands like the garden of the LORD. Joy and gladness will be found in her, thanksgiving and the sound of singing.

Isaiah 55:10-11

As the rain and the snow come down from heaven, and do not return to it without watering the earth and making it bud and flourish, so that it yields seed for the sower and bread for the eater, so is my word that goes out from my mouth: It will not return to me empty, but will accomplish what I desire and achieve the purpose for which I sent it.

Jeremiah 17:7-8

"But blessed is the one who trusts in the LORD, whose confidence is in him. They will be like a tree planted by the water that sends out its roots by the stream. It does not fear when heat comes; its leaves are always green. It has no worries in a year of drought and never fails to bear fruit."

Ezekiel 44:30

The best of all the firstfruits and of all your special gifts will belong to the priests. You are to give them the first portion of your ground meal so that a blessing may rest on your household.

Micah 4:11-13

But now many nations are gathered against you. They say, "Let her be defiled, let our eyes gloat over Zion!" But they do not know the thoughts of the LORD; they do not understand his plan, that he has gathered them like sheaves to the threshing floor. "Rise and thresh, Daughter Zion, for I will give you horns of iron; I will give you hooves of bronze, and you will break to pieces many nations." You will devote their ill-gotten gains to the LORD, their wealth to the Lord of all the earth.

Haggai 2:8-9

"The silver is mine and the gold is mine," declares the LORD Almighty. "The glory of this present house will be greater than the glory of the former house," says the LORD Almighty. "And in this place I will grant peace," declares the LORD Almighty.

Zechariah 8:13

Just as you, Judah and Israel, have been a curse among the nations, so I will save you, and you will be a blessing. Do not be afraid, but let your hands be strong."

Malachi 3:8-12

"Will a mere mortal rob God? Yet you rob me. "But you ask, 'How are we robbing you?' "In tithes and offerings. You are under a curse—your whole nation—because you are robbing me. Bring the whole tithe into the storehouse, that there may be food in my house. Test me in this," says the LORD Almighty, "and see if I will not throw open the floodgates of heaven and pour out so much blessing that there will not be room enough to store it. I will prevent pests from devouring your crops, and the vines in your fields will not drop their fruit before it is ripe," says the LORD Almighty. "Then all the nations will call you blessed, for yours will be a delightful land," says the LORD Almighty.

NEW TESTAMENT

Matthew 6:24

"No one can serve two masters. Either you will hate the one and love the other, or you will be devoted to the one and despise the other. You cannot serve both God and money.

Matthew 12:25-29

Jesus knew their thoughts and said to them, "Every kingdom divided against itself will be ruined, and every city or household divided against itself will not stand. If Satan drives out Satan, he is divided against himself. How then can his kingdom stand? And if I drive out demons by Beelzebul, by whom do your people drive them out? So then, they will be your judges. But if it is by the Spirit of God that I drive out demons, then the kingdom of God has come upon you. "Or again, how can anyone enter a strong man's house and carry off his possessions unless he first ties up the strong man? Then he can plunder his house.

Matthew 24:45-47

"Who then is the faithful and wise servant, whom the master has put in charge of the servants in his household to give them their food at the proper time? It will be good for that servant whose master finds him doing so when he returns. Truly I tell you, he will put him in charge of all his possessions.

Luke 1:45

Blessed is she who has believed that the Lord would fulfill his promises to her!"

Luke 6:20

Looking at his disciples, he said: "Blessed are you who are poor, for yours is the kingdom of God.

Luke 11:23

"Whoever is not with me is against me, and whoever does not gather with me scatters.

John 20:29

Then Jesus told him, "Because you have seen me, you have believed; blessed are those who have not seen and yet have believed."

Acts 20:32-35

"Now I commit you to God and to the word of his grace, which can build you up and give you an inheritance among all those who are sanctified. I have not coveted anyone's silver or gold or clothing. You yourselves know that these hands of mine have supplied my own needs and the needs of my companions. In everything I did, I showed you that by this kind of hard work we must help the weak, remembering the words the Lord Jesus himself said: 'It is more blessed to give than to receive.'"

Galatians 3:6-9

So also Abraham "believed God, and it was credited to him as righteousness." Understand, then, that those who have faith are children of Abraham. Scripture foresaw that God would justify the Gentiles by faith, and announced the gospel in advance to Abraham: "All nations will be blessed through you." So those who rely on faith are blessed along with Abraham, the man of faith.

Galatians 3:13, 14

Christ redeemed us from the curse of the law by becoming a curse for us, for it is written: "Cursed is everyone who is hung on a pole." He redeemed us in order that the blessing given to Abraham might come to the Gentiles through Christ Jesus, so that by faith we might receive the promise of the Spirit.

Ephesians 1:3

Praise be to the God and Father of our Lord Jesus Christ, who has blessed us in the heavenly realms with every spiritual blessing in Christ.

Ephesians 4:28

Anyone who has been stealing must steal no longer, but must work, doing something useful with their own hands, that they may have something to share with those in need.

2 Thessalonians 2:16, 17

May our Lord Jesus Christ himself and God our Father, who loved us and by his grace gave us eternal encouragement and good hope, encourage your hearts and strengthen you in every good deed and word.

2 Thessalonians 3:6-10

In the name of the Lord Jesus Christ, we command you, brothers and sisters, to keep away from every believer who is idle and disruptive and does not live according to the teaching you received from us. For you yourselves know how you ought to follow our example. We were not idle when we were with you, nor did we eat anyone's food without paying for it. On the contrary, we worked night and day, laboring and toiling so that we would not be a burden to any of you. We did this, not because we do not have the right to such help, but in order to offer ourselves as a model for you to imitate. For even when we were with you, we gave you this rule: "The one who is unwilling to work shall not eat."

Hebrews 7:1-6

This Melchizedek was king of Salem and priest of God Most High. He met Abraham returning from the defeat of the kings and blessed him, and Abraham gave him a tenth of everything. First, the name Melchizedek means "king of righteousness"; then also, "king of Salem" means "king of peace." Without father or mother, without genealogy, without beginning of days or end of life, resembling the Son of God, he remains a priest forever.

Just think how great he was: Even the patriarch Abraham gave him a tenth of the plunder! Now the law requires the descendants of Levi who become priests to collect a tenth from the people—that is, from their fellow Israelites—even though they also are descended from Abraham. This man, however, did not trace his descent from Levi, yet he collected a tenth from Abraham and blessed him who had the promises.

James 1:22-25

Do not merely listen to the word, and so deceive yourselves. Do what it says. Anyone who listens to the word but does not do what it says is like someone who looks at his face in a mirror and, after looking at himself, goes away and immediately forgets what he looks like. But whoever looks intently into the perfect law that gives freedom, and continues in it—not forgetting what they have heard, but doing it—they will be blessed in what they do.

1 Peter 3:8-11

Finally, all of you, be like-minded, be sympathetic, love one another, be compassionate and humble. Do not repay evil with evil or insult with insult. On the contrary, repay evil with blessing, because to this you were called so that you may inherit a blessing. For, "Whoever would love life and see good days must keep their tongue from evil and their lips from deceitful speech. They must turn from evil and do good; they must seek peace and pursue it.

3 John 1:2

Dear friend, I pray that you may enjoy good health and that all may go well with you, even as your soul is getting along well.

CHAPTER ELEVEN

Scripture Keys for Favor

OLD TESTAMENT

Genesis 30:27-30

But Laban said to him, "If I have found favor in your eyes, please stay. I have learned by divination that the LORD has blessed me because of you." He added, "Name your wages, and I will pay them."

Jacob said to him, "You know how I have worked for you and how your livestock has fared under my care. The little you had before I came has increased greatly, and the LORD has blessed you wherever I have been. But now, when may I do something for my own household?"

Genesis 39:2-6

The LORD was with Joseph so that he prospered, and he lived in the house of his Egyptian master. When his master saw that the LORD was with him and that the LORD gave him success in everything he did, Joseph found favor in his eyes and became his attendant. Potiphar put him in charge of his household, and he entrusted to his care everything he owned. From the time he put him in charge of his household and of all that he owned, the LORD blessed the household of the Egyptian because of Joseph. The blessing of the LORD was on everything Potiphar had, both in the house and in the field. So Potiphar left everything he had in Joseph's care; with Joseph in charge, he did not concern himself with anything except the food he ate.

Genesis 39:20-23

Joseph's master took him and put him in prison, the place where the king's prisoners were confined.

But while Joseph was there in the prison, the LORD was with him; he showed him kindness and granted him favor in the eyes of the prison warden. So the warden put Joseph in charge of all those held in the prison, and he was made responsible for all that was done there. The warden paid no attention to anything under Joseph's care, because the LORD was with Joseph and gave him success in whatever he did.

Exodus 3:21, 22

"And I will make the Egyptians favorably disposed toward this people, so that when you leave you will not go empty-handed. Every woman is to ask her neighbor and any woman living in her house for articles of silver and gold and for clothing, which you will put on your sons and daughters. And so you will plunder the Egyptians."

Exodus 12:36

The LORD had made the Egyptians favorably disposed toward the people, and they gave them what they asked for; so they plundered the Egyptians.

Deuteronomy 16:17

Each of you must bring a gift in proportion to the way the LORD your God has blessed you.

Deuteronomy 23:21

If you make a vow to the LORD your God, do not be slow to pay it, for the LORD your God will certainly demand it of you and you will be guilty of sin.

Deuteronomy 29:9

Carefully follow the terms of this covenant, so that you may prosper in everything you do.

Joshus 22:8

"Return to your homes with your great wealth—with large herds of livestock, with silver, gold, bronze and iron, and a great quantity of clothing—and divide the plunder from your enemies with your fellow Israelites."

Judges 18:5

Then they said to him, "Please inquire of God to learn whether our journey will be successful."

Ruth 2:12

"May the LORD repay you for what you have done. May you be richly rewarded by the LORD, the God of Israel, under whose wings you have come to take refuge."

1 Samuel 2:7-10

The LORD sends poverty and wealth; he humbles and he exalts.

He raises the poor from the dust and lifts the needy from the ash heap; he seats them with princes and has them inherit a throne of honor.

"For the foundations of the earth are the LORD's; on them he has set the world. He will guard the feet of his faithful servants, but the wicked will be silenced in the place of darkness.

"It is not by strength that one prevails; those who oppose the LORD will be broken. The Most High will thunder from heaven; the LORD will judge the ends of the earth.

"He will give strength to his king and exalt the horn of his anointed."

1 Kings 3:11-13

So God said to him, "Since you have asked for this and not for long life or wealth for yourself, nor have asked for the death of your enemies but for discernment in administering justice, I will do what you have asked. I will give you a wise and discerning heart, so that there will never have been anyone like you, nor will there ever be. Moreover, I will give you what you have not asked for—both wealth and honor—so that in your lifetime you will have no equal among kings."

1 Chronicles 17:23-27

"And now, LORD, let the promise you have made concerning your servant and his house be established forever.

Do as you promised, so that it will be established and that your name will be great forever. Then people will say, 'The LORD Almighty, the God over Israel, is Israel's God!' And the house of your servant David will be established before you.

"You, my God, have revealed to your servant that you will build a house for him. So your servant has found courage to pray to you. You, LORD, are God! You have promised these good things to your servant. Now you have been pleased to bless the house of your servant, that it may continue forever in your sight; for you, LORD, have blessed it, and it will be blessed forever."

1 Chronicles 29:12

Wealth and honor come from you; you are the ruler of all things. In your hands are strength and power to exalt and give strength to all.

2 Chronicles 1:11, 12

God said to Solomon, "Since this is your heart's desire and you have not asked for wealth, possessions or honor, nor for the death of your enemies, and since you have not asked for a long life but for wisdom and knowledge to govern my people over whom I have made you king, therefore wisdom and knowledge will be given you. And I will also give you wealth, possessions and honor, such as no king who was before you ever had and none after you will have."

2 Chronicles 17:3-6

The LORD was with Jehoshaphat because he followed the ways of his father David before him. He did not consult the Baals but sought the God of his father and followed his commands rather than the practices of Israel. The LORD established the kingdom under his control; and all Judah brought gifts to Jehoshaphat, so that he had great wealth and honor. His heart was devoted to the ways of the LORD; furthermore, he removed the high places and the Asherah poles from Judah.

2 Chronicles 26:5

He sought God during the days of Zechariah, who instructed him in the fear of God. As long as he sought the LORD, God gave him success.

2 Chronicles 32:27-30

Hezekiah had very great wealth and honor, and he made treasuries for his silver and gold and for his precious stones, spices, shields and all kinds of valuables. He also made buildings to store the harvest of grain, new wine and olive oil; and he made stalls for various kinds of cattle, and pens for the flocks. He built villages and acquired great numbers of flocks and herds, for God had given him very great riches.

It was Hezekiah who blocked the upper outlet of the Gihon spring and channeled the water down to the west side of the City of David. He succeeded in everything he undertook.

Nehemiah 2:20

I answered them by saying, "The God of heaven will give us success. We his servants will start rebuilding, but as for you, you have no share in Jerusalem or any claim or historic right to it."

Job 29:1-25

Job continued his discourse:

"How I long for the months gone by, for the days when God watched over me, when his lamp shone on my head and by his light I walked through darkness! Oh, for the days when I was in my prime, when God's intimate friendship blessed my house, when the Almighty was still with me and my children were around me, when my path was drenched with cream and the rock poured out for me streams of olive oil.

"When I went to the gate of the city and took my seat in the public square, the young men saw me and stepped aside and the old men rose to their feet; the chief men refrained from speaking and covered their mouths with their hands; the voices of the nobles were hushed, and their tongues stuck to the roof of their mouths. Whoever heard me spoke well of me, and those who saw me commended me, because I rescued the poor who cried for help, and the fatherless who had none to assist them. The one who was dying blessed me; I made the widow's heart sing. I put on righteousness as my clothing; justice was my robe and my turban. I was eyes to the blind and feet to the lame. I was a father to the needy; I took up the case of the stranger. I broke the fangs of the wicked and snatched the victims from their teeth.

"I thought, 'I will die in my own house, my days as numerous as the grains of sand. My roots will reach to the water, and the dew will lie all night on my branches. My glory will not fade; the bow will be ever new in my hand.'

"People listened to me expectantly, waiting in silence for my counsel. After I had spoken, they spoke no more; my words fell gently on their ears. They waited for me as for showers and drank in my words as the spring rain. When I smiled at them, they scarcely believed it; the light of my face was precious to them. I chose the way for them and sat as their chief; I dwelt as a king among his troops; I was like one who comforts mourners.

Job 36:7-11

He does not take his eyes off the righteous; he enthrones them with kings and exalts them forever.

But if people are bound in chains, held fast by cords of affliction, he tells them what they have done—that they have sinned arrogantly.

He makes them listen to correction and commands them to repent of their evil.

If they obey and serve him, they will spend the rest of their days in prosperity and their years in contentment.

Job 36:15, 16

But those who suffer he delivers in their suffering; he speaks to them in their affliction.

"He is wooing you from the jaws of distress to a spacious place free from restriction, to the comfort of your table laden with choice food.

Psalm 5:11, 12

But let all who take refuge in you be glad; let them ever sing for joy. Spread your protection over them, that those who love your name may rejoice in you. Surely, LORD, you bless the righteous; you surround them with your favor as with a shield.

Psalm 23:1-6

The LORD is my shepherd, I lack nothing.

He makes me lie down in green pastures, he leads me beside quiet waters, he refreshes my soul. He guides me along the right paths for his name's sake.

Even though I walk through the darkest valley, I will fear no evil, for you are with me; your rod and your staff, they comfort me.

You prepare a table before me in the presence of my enemies.

You anoint my head with oil; my cup overflows.

Surely your goodness and love will follow me all the days of my life, and I will dwell in the house of the LORD forever.

Psalm 106:3-5

Blessed are those who act justly, who always do what is right. Remember me, LORD, when you show favor to your people, come to my aid when you save them, that I may enjoy the prosperity of your chosen ones, that I may share in the joy of your nation and join your inheritance in giving praise.

Psalm 112:3-4, AMP

Prosperity and welfare are in his house, and his righteousness endures forever. Light arises in the darkness for the upright, gracious, compassionate, and just [who are in right standing with God].

Psalm 112:5-9

> Good will come to those who are generous and lend freely, who conduct their affairs with justice. Surely the righteous will never be shaken; they will be remembered forever.

> They will have no fear of bad news; their hearts are steadfast, trusting in the LORD. Their hearts are secure, they will have no fear; in the end they will look in triumph on their foes.

> They have freely scattered their gifts to the poor, their righteousness endures forever; their horn will be lifted high in honor.

Psalm 113:7, 8

> He raises the poor from the dust and lifts the needy from the ash heap; he seats them with princes, with the princes of his people.

Proverbs 3:1-8

> My son, do not forget my teaching, but keep my commands in your heart, for they will prolong your life many years and bring you peace and prosperity.

> Let love and faithfulness never leave you; bind them around your neck, write them on the tablet of your heart. Then you will win favor and a good name in the sight of God and man.

> Trust in the LORD with all your heart and lean not on your own understanding; in all your ways submit to him, and he will make your paths straight.

Do not be wise in your own eyes; fear the LORD and shun evil. This will bring health to your body and nourishment to your bones.

Proverbs 8:12

I, wisdom, dwell together with prudence; I possess knowledge and discretion.

Proverbs 8:18-21

With me are riches and honor, enduring wealth and prosperity. My fruit is better than fine gold; what I yield surpasses choice silver.

I walk in the way of righteousness, along the paths of justice, bestowing a rich inheritance on those who love me and making their treasuries full.

Proverbs 8:35

For those who find me find life and receive favor from the LORD.

Proverbs 11:27, 28

Whoever seeks good finds favor, but evil comes to one who searches for it. Those who trust in their riches will fall, but the righteous will thrive like a green leaf.

Proverbs 13:18

Whoever disregards discipline comes to poverty and shame, but whoever heeds correction is honored.

Proverbs 15:6

The house of the righteous contains great treasure, but the income of the wicked brings ruin.

Proverbs 18:16

A gift opens the way and ushers the giver into the presence of the great.

Proverbs 19:6

Many curry favor with a ruler, and everyone is the friend of one who gives gifts.

Proverbs 21:20

The wise store up choice food and olive oil, but fools gulp theirs down.

Proverbs 22:1

A good name is more desirable than great riches; to be esteemed is better than silver or gold.

Proverbs 22:4

Humility is the fear of the LORD; its wages are riches and honor and life.

Proverbs 22:7

The rich rule over the poor, and the borrower is slave to the lender.

Proverbs 22:29

Do you see someone skilled in their work? They will serve before kings; they will not serve before officials of low rank.

Isaiah 32:17-20

The fruit of that righteousness will be peace; its effect will be quietness and confidence forever. My people will live in peaceful dwelling places, in secure homes, in undisturbed places of rest.

Though hail flattens the forest and the city is leveled completely, how blessed you will be, sowing your seed by every stream, and letting your cattle and donkeys range free.

Jeremiah 29:11

"For I know the plans I have for you," declares the LORD, "plans to prosper you and not to harm you, plans to give you hope and a future."

Jeremiah 33:7-9

I will bring Judah and Israel back from captivity and will rebuild them as they were before. I will cleanse them from all the sin they have committed against me and will forgive all their sins of rebellion against me. Then this city will bring me renown, joy, praise and honor before all nations on earth that hear of all the good things I do for it; and they will be in awe and will tremble at the abundant prosperity and peace I provide for it.

Malachi 3:8-12

"Will a mere mortal rob God? Yet you rob me.

"But you ask, 'How are we robbing you?'

"In tithes and offerings. You are under a curse—your whole nation—because you are robbing me. Bring the whole tithe into the storehouse, that there may be food in my house. Test me in this," says the LORD Almighty, "and see if I will not throw open the floodgates of heaven and pour out so much blessing that there will not be room enough to store it. I will prevent pests from devouring your crops, and the vines in your fields will not drop their fruit before it is ripe," says the LORD Almighty. "Then all the nations will

call you blessed, for yours will be a delightful land," says the
LORD Almighty.

NEW TESTAMENT

Matthew 6:33, AMP

But seek (aim at and strive after) first of all His kingdom
and His righteousness (His way of doing and being right),
and then all these things taken together will be given you
besides.

Matthew 7:7-11

"Ask and it will be given to you; seek and you will find;
knock and the door will be opened to you. For everyone
who asks receives; the one who seeks finds; and to the one
who knocks, the door will be opened.

"Which of you, if your son asks for bread, will give him a
stone? Or if he asks for a fish, will give him a snake? If you,
then, though you are evil, know how to give good gifts to
your children, how much more will your Father in heaven
give good gifts to those who ask him!

Matthew 17:19-20

Then the disciples came to Jesus in private and asked, "Why
couldn't we drive it out?"

He replied, "Because you have so little faith. Truly I tell you,
if you have faith as small as a mustard seed, you can say to
this mountain, 'Move from here to there,' and it will move.
Nothing will be impossible for you."

Mark 11:22-25

"Have faith in God," Jesus answered. "Truly I tell you, if anyone says to this mountain, 'Go, throw yourself into the sea,' and does not doubt in their heart but believes that what they say will happen, it will be done for them. Therefore I tell you, whatever you ask for in prayer, believe that you have received it, and it will be yours. And when you stand praying, if you hold anything against anyone, forgive them, so that your Father in heaven may forgive you your sins."

Luke 6:20

Looking at his disciples, he said:

"Blessed are you who are poor, for yours is the kingdom of God.

Luke 6:38

Give, and it will be given to you. A good measure, pressed down, shaken together and running over, will be poured into your lap. For with the measure you use, it will be measured to you."

Luke 10:18-20

He replied, "I saw Satan fall like lightning from heaven. I have given you authority to trample on snakes and scorpions and to overcome all the power of the enemy; nothing will harm you. However, do not rejoice that the spirits submit to you, but rejoice that your names are written in heaven."

Luke 11:5-13

Then Jesus said to them, "Suppose you have a friend, and you go to him at midnight and say, 'Friend, lend me three loaves of bread; a friend of mine on a journey has come to me, and I have no food to offer him.' And suppose the one inside answers, 'Don't bother me. The door is already locked, and my children and I are in bed. I can't get up and give you anything.' I tell you, even though he will not get up and give you the bread because of friendship, yet because of your shameless audacity he will surely get up and give you as much as you need.

"So I say to you: Ask and it will be given to you; seek and you will find; knock and the door will be opened to you. For everyone who asks receives; the one who seeks finds; and to the one who knocks, the door will be opened.

"Which of you fathers, if your son asks for a fish, will give him a snake instead? Or if he asks for an egg, will give him a scorpion? If you then, though you are evil, know how to give good gifts to your children, how much more will your Father in heaven give the Holy Spirit to those who ask him!"

John 14:13, 14

And I will do whatever you ask in my name, so that the Father may be glorified in the Son. You may ask me for anything in my name, and I will do it.

John 14:26, 27

But the Advocate, the Holy Spirit, whom the Father will send in my name, will teach you all things and will remind you of everything I have said to you. Peace I leave with you; my peace I give you. I do not give to you as the world gives. Do not let your hearts be troubled and do not be afraid.

John 16:23-27

In that day you will no longer ask me anything. Very truly I tell you, my Father will give you whatever you ask in my name. Until now you have not asked for anything in my name. Ask and you will receive, and your joy will be complete.

"Though I have been speaking figuratively, a time is coming when I will no longer use this kind of language but will tell you plainly about my Father. In that day you will ask in my name. I am not saying that I will ask the Father on your behalf. No, the Father himself loves you because you have loved me and have believed that I came from God.

Romans 5:17

For if, by the trespass of the one man, death reigned through that one man, how much more will those who receive God's abundant provision of grace and of the gift of righteousness reign in life through the one man, Jesus Christ!

Romans 8:31, 32

What, then, shall we say in response to these things? If God is for us, who can be against us? He who did not spare his own Son, but gave him up for us all—how will he not also, along with him, graciously give us all things?

1 Corinthians 15:58

Therefore, my dear brothers and sisters, stand firm. Let nothing move you. Always give yourselves fully to the work of the Lord, because you know that your labor in the Lord is not in vain.

2 Corinthians 6:10

...sorrowful, yet always rejoicing; poor, yet making many rich; having nothing, and yet possessing everything.

2 Corinthians 8:2-5

In the midst of a very severe trial, their overflowing joy and their extreme poverty welled up in rich generosity. For I testify that they gave as much as they were able, and even beyond their ability. Entirely on their own, they urgently pleaded with us for the privilege of sharing in this service to the Lord's people. And they exceeded our expectations: They gave themselves first of all to the Lord, and then by the will of God also to us.

2 Corinthians 8:12-14

For if the willingness is there, the gift is acceptable according to what one has, not according to what one does not have.

Our desire is not that others might be relieved while you are hard pressed, but that there might be equality. At the present time your plenty will supply what they need, so that in turn their plenty will supply what you need. The goal is equality.

2 Corinthians 9:7

Each of you should give what you have decided in your heart to give, not reluctantly or under compulsion, for God loves a cheerful giver.

Philippians 4:10-19

I rejoiced greatly in the Lord that at last you renewed your concern for me. Indeed, you were concerned, but you had no opportunity to show it. I am not saying this because I am in need, for I have learned to be content whatever the circumstances. I know what it is to be in need, and I know what it is to have plenty. I have learned the secret of being content in any and every situation, whether well fed or hungry, whether living in plenty or in want. I can do all this through him who gives me strength.

Yet it was good of you to share in my troubles. Moreover, as you Philippians know, in the early days of your acquaintance with the gospel, when I set out from Macedonia, not one church shared with me in the matter of giving and receiving, except you only; for even when I was in Thessalonica, you sent me aid more than once when I was in need. Not that I desire your gifts; what I desire is that more be credited to your account. I have received full payment and have more than enough. I am amply supplied, now that I have received from Epaphroditus the gifts you sent. They are a fragrant offering, an acceptable sacrifice, pleasing to God. And my God will meet all your needs according to the riches of his glory in Christ Jesus.

Colossians 4:1

Masters, provide your slaves with what is right and fair, because you know that you also have a Master in heaven.

2 Thessalonians 1:11, 12

With this in mind, we constantly pray for you, that our God may make you worthy of his calling, and that by his power he may bring to fruition your every desire for goodness and your every deed prompted by faith. We pray this so that the name of our Lord Jesus may be glorified in you, and you in him, according to the grace of our God and the Lord Jesus Christ.

1 Timothy 4:14, 15

Do not neglect your gift, which was given you through prophecy when the body of elders laid their hands on you.

Be diligent in these matters; give yourself wholly to them, so that everyone may see your progress.

Hebrews 11:1-3

Now faith is confidence in what we hope for and assurance about what we do not see. This is what the ancients were commended for.

By faith we understand that the universe was formed at God's command, so that what is seen was not made out of what was visible.

Hebrews 11:6

And without faith it is impossible to please God, because anyone who comes to him must believe that he exists and that he rewards those who earnestly seek him.

Hebrews 13:5, 6

Keep your lives free from the love of money and be content with what you have, because God has said,

"Never will I leave you; never will I forsake you."

So we say with confidence,

"The Lord is my helper; I will not be afraid. What can mere mortals do to me?"

James 1:5-8

If any of you lacks wisdom, you should ask God, who gives generously to all without finding fault, and it will be given to you. But when you ask, you must believe and not doubt, because the one who doubts is like a wave of the sea, blown and tossed by the wind. That person should not expect to receive anything from the Lord. Such a person is double-minded and unstable in all they do.

James 4:10

Humble yourselves before the Lord, and he will lift you up.

Revelation 2:9

I know your afflictions and your poverty—yet you are rich! I know about the slander of those who say they are Jews and are not, but are a synagogue of Satan.

CHAPTER TWELVE

SCRIPTURE KEYS FOR INCREASE

OLD TESTAMENT

Genesis 8:22

"As long as the earth endures, seedtime and harvest, cold and heat, summer and winter, day and night will never cease."

Genesis 13:5, 6

Now Lot, who was moving about with Abram, also had flocks and herds and tents. But the land could not support them while they stayed together, for their possessions were so great that they were not able to stay together.

Genesis 15:13, 14

Then the LORD said to him, "Know for certain that for four hundred years your descendants will be strangers in a country not their own and that they will be enslaved and mistreated there. But I will punish the nation they serve as slaves, and afterward they will come out with great possessions.

Genesis 26:2-5

The LORD appeared to Isaac and said, "Do not go down to Egypt; live in the land where I tell you to live. Stay in this land for a while, and I will be with you and will bless you. For to you and your descendants I will give all these lands and will confirm the oath I swore to your father Abraham. I will make your descendants as numerous as the stars in the sky and will give them all these lands, and through your offspring all nations on earth will be blessed, because Abraham obeyed me and did everything I required of him, keeping my commands, my decrees and my instructions."

Genesis 26:12-14

Isaac planted crops in that land and the same year reaped a hundredfold, because the LORD blessed him. The man became rich, and his wealth continued to grow until he became very wealthy. He had so many flocks and herds and servants that the Philistines envied him.

Genesis 28:3, 4

May God Almighty bless you and make you fruitful and increase your numbers until you become a community of peoples. May he give you and your descendants the blessing given to Abraham, so that you may take possession of the land where you now reside as a foreigner, the land God gave to Abraham."

Genesis 30:27-30

But Laban said to him, "If I have found favor in your eyes, please stay. I have learned by divination that the LORD has blessed me because of you." He added, "Name your wages, and I will pay them."

Jacob said to him, "You know how I have worked for you and how your livestock has fared under my care. The little you had before I came has increased greatly, and the LORD has blessed you wherever I have been. But now, when may I do something for my own household?"

Genesis 36:6, 7

Esau took his wives and sons and daughters and all the members of his household, as well as his livestock and all his other animals and all the goods he had acquired in Canaan, and moved to a land some distance from his brother Jacob. Their possessions were too great for them to remain together; the land where they were staying could not support them both because of their livestock.

Leviticus 19:9, 10

When you reap the harvest of your land, do not reap to the very edges of your field or gather the gleanings of your harvest. Do not go over your vineyard a second time or pick up the grapes that have fallen. Leave them for the poor and the foreigner. I am the LORD your God.

Leviticus 23:10

"Speak to the Israelites and say to them: 'When you enter the land I am going to give you and you reap its harvest, bring to the priest a sheaf of the first grain you harvest.'"

Leviticus 26:3-13

"If you follow my decrees and are careful to obey my commands, I will send you rain in its season, and the ground will yield its crops and the trees their fruit. Your threshing will continue until grape harvest and the grape harvest will continue until planting, and you will eat all the food you want and live in safety in your land.

"I will grant peace in the land, and you will lie down and no one will make you afraid. I will remove wild beasts from the land, and the sword will not pass through your country. You will pursue your enemies, and they will fall by the sword before you. Five of you will chase a hundred, and a hundred of you will chase ten thousand, and your enemies will fall by the sword before you.

"I will look on you with favor and make you fruitful and increase your numbers, and I will keep my covenant with you. You will still be eating last year's harvest when you will have to move it out to make room for the new. I will put my dwelling place among you, and I will not abhor you. I will walk among you and be your God, and you will be my people. I am the LORD your God, who brought you out of Egypt so that you would no longer be slaves to the Egyptians; I broke the bars of your yoke and enabled you to walk with heads held high."

Deuteronomy 8:18

But remember the LORD your God, for it is he who gives you the ability to produce wealth, and so confirms his covenant, which he swore to your ancestors, as it is today.

Deuteronomy 11:13-15

So if you faithfully obey the commands I am giving you today—to love the LORD your God and to serve him with all your heart and with all your soul— then I will send rain on your land in its season, both autumn and spring rains, so that you may gather in your grain, new wine and olive oil. I will provide grass in the fields for your cattle, and you will eat and be satisfied.

Deuteronomy 11:18-28

Fix these words of mine in your hearts and minds; tie them as symbols on your hands and bind them on your foreheads. Teach them to your children, talking about them when you sit at home and when you walk along the road, when you lie down and when you get up. Write them on the doorframes of your houses and on your gates, so that your days and the days of your children may be many in the land the LORD swore to give your ancestors, as many as the days that the heavens are above the earth.

If you carefully observe all these commands I am giving you to follow—to love the LORD your God, to walk in obedience to him and to hold fast to him— then the LORD will drive out all these nations before you, and you will dispossess nations larger and stronger than you. Every place where you set your foot will be yours: Your territory will extend from the desert to Lebanon, and from the Euphrates River to the Mediterranean Sea. No one will be able to stand against you. The LORD your God, as he promised you, will put the terror and fear of you on the whole land, wherever you go.

See, I am setting before you today a blessing and a curse—the blessing if you obey the commands of the LORD your God that I am giving you today; the curse if you disobey the commands of the LORD your God and turn from the way that I command you today by following other gods, which you have not known.

Deuteronomy 14:22-29

Be sure to set aside a tenth of all that your fields produce each year. Eat the tithe of your grain, new wine and olive oil, and the firstborn of your herds and flocks in the presence of the LORD your God at the place he will choose as a dwelling for his Name, so that you may learn to revere the LORD your God always. But if that place is too distant and you have been blessed by the LORD your God and cannot carry your tithe (because the place where the LORD will choose to put his Name is so far away), then exchange your tithe for silver, and take the silver with you and go to the place the LORD your God will choose. Use the silver to buy whatever you like: cattle, sheep, wine or other fermented drink, or anything you wish. Then you and your household shall eat there in the presence of the LORD your God and rejoice. And do not neglect the Levites living in your towns, for they have no allotment or inheritance of their own.

At the end of every three years, bring all the tithes of that year's produce and store it in your towns, so that the Levites (who have no allotment or inheritance of their own) and the foreigners, the fatherless and the widows who live in your towns may come and eat and be satisfied, and so that the LORD your God may bless you in all the work of your hands.

Job 1:3

And he owned seven thousand sheep, three thousand camels, five hundred yoke of oxen and five hundred donkeys, and had a large number of servants. He was the greatest man among all the people of the East.

Job 1:10

"Have you not put a hedge around him and his household and everything he has? You have blessed the work of his hands, so that his flocks and herds are spread throughout the land."

Job 8:6, 7

If you are pure and upright, even now he will rouse himself on your behalf and restore you to your prosperous state. Your beginnings will seem humble, so prosperous will your future be.

Job 22:21-30

"Submit to God and be at peace with him; in this way prosperity will come to you. Accept instruction from his mouth and lay up his words in your heart. If you return to the Almighty, you will be restored: If you remove wickedness far from your tent and assign your nuggets to the dust, your gold of Ophir to the rocks in the ravines, then the Almighty will be your gold, the choicest silver for you. Surely then you will find delight in the Almighty and will lift up your face to God. You will pray to him, and he will hear you, and you will fulfill your vows. What you decide on will be done, and light will shine on your ways. When people are brought low and you say, 'Lift them up!' then he will save the downcast. He will deliver even one who is not innocent, who will be delivered through the cleanness of your hands."

Job 22:28 (AMP)

You shall also decide and decree a thing, and it shall be established for you; and the light [of God's favor] shall shine upon your ways.

Job 42:10-12

After Job had prayed for his friends, the LORD restored his fortunes and gave him twice as much as he had before. All his brothers and sisters and everyone who had known him before came and ate with him in his house. They comforted and consoled him over all the trouble the LORD had brought on him, and each one gave him a piece of silver and a gold ring. The LORD blessed the latter part of Job's life more than the former part. He had fourteen thousand sheep, six thousand camels, a thousand yoke of oxen and a thousand donkeys.

Psalm 23:5 (AMP)

You prepare a table before me in the presence of my enemies. You anoint my head with oil; my [brimming] cup runs over.

Psalm 85:12, 13

The LORD will indeed give what is good, and our land will yield its harvest. Righteousness goes before him and prepares the way for his steps.

Psalm 104:24

How many are your works, LORD! In wisdom you made them all; the earth is full of your creatures.

Psalm 112:2

Their children will be mighty in the land; the generation of the upright will be blessed.

Psalm 115:14

May the LORD cause you to flourish, both you and your children.

Psalm 126:4-6

Restore our fortunes, LORD, like streams in the Negev. Those who sow with tears will reap with songs of joy. Those who go out weeping, carrying seed to sow, will return with songs of joy, carrying sheaves with them.

Proverbs 3:27, 28

Do not withhold good from those to whom it is due, when it is in your power to act. Do not say to your neighbor, "Come back tomorrow and I'll give it to you"— when you already have it with you.

Proverbs 6:30, 31

People do not despise a thief if he steals to satisfy his hunger when he is starving. Yet if he is caught, he must pay sevenfold, though it costs him all the wealth of his house.

Proverbs 10:3-5

The LORD does not let the righteous go hungry, but he thwarts the craving of the wicked. Lazy hands make for poverty, but diligent hands bring wealth. He who gathers crops in summer is a prudent son, but he who sleeps during harvest is a disgraceful son.

Proverbs 10:14, 15

The wise store up knowledge, but the mouth of a fool invites ruin. The wealth of the rich is their fortified city, but poverty is the ruin of the poor.

Proverbs 11:23-25

The desire of the righteous ends only in good, but the hope of the wicked only in wrath. One person gives freely, yet gains even more; another withholds unduly, but comes to poverty. A generous person will prosper; whoever refreshes others will be refreshed.

Proverbs 12:11

Those who work their land will have abundant food, but those who chase fantasies have no sense.

Proverbs 12:14

From the fruit of their lips people are filled with good things, and the work of their hands brings them reward.

Proverbs 12:24

Diligent hands will rule, but laziness ends in forced labor.

Proverbs 12:27

The lazy do not roast any game, but the diligent feed on the riches of the hunt.

Proverbs 13:2-4

From the fruit of their lips people enjoy good things, but the unfaithful have an appetite for violence. Those who guard their lips preserve their lives, but those who speak rashly will come to ruin. A sluggard's appetite is never filled, but the desires of the diligent are fully satisfied.

Proverbs 13:11

Dishonest money dwindles away, but whoever gathers money little by little makes it grow.

Proverbs 13:22

A good person leaves an inheritance for their children's children, but a sinner's wealth is stored up for the righteous.

Proverbs 14:4

Where there are no oxen, the manger is empty, but from the strength of an ox come abundant harvests.

Proverbs 14:31

Whoever oppresses the poor shows contempt for their Maker, but whoever is kind to the needy honors God.

Proverbs 15:6

The house of the righteous contains great treasure, but the income of the wicked brings ruin.

Proverbs 17:8

A bribe is seen as a charm by the one who gives it; they think success will come at every turn.

Proverbs 19:17

Whoever is kind to the poor lends to the LORD, and he will reward them for what they have done.

Proverbs 22:9

The generous will themselves be blessed, for they share their food with the poor.

Proverbs 22:22, 23

Do not exploit the poor because they are poor and do not crush the needy in court, for the LORD will take up their case and will exact life for life.

Proverbs 23:4, 5

Do not wear yourself out to get rich; do not trust your own cleverness. Cast but a glance at riches, and they are gone, for they will surely sprout wings and fly off to the sky like an eagle.

Proverbs 28:25-27

The greedy stir up conflict, but those who trust in the LORD will prosper. Those who trust in themselves are fools, but those who walk in wisdom are kept safe. Those who give to the poor will lack nothing, but those who close their eyes to them receive many curses.

Ecclesiastes 5:3

A dream comes when there are many cares, and many words mark the speech of a fool.

Ecclesiastes 5:9-11

The increase from the land is taken by all; the king himself profits from the fields. Whoever loves money never has enough; whoever loves wealth is never satisfied with their income. This too is meaningless. As goods increase, so do those who consume them. And what benefit are they to the owners except to feast their eyes on them?

Ecclesiastes 5:12, 13

The sleep of a laborer is sweet, whether they eat little or much, but as for the rich, their abundance permits them no sleep. I have seen a grievous evil under the sun: wealth hoarded to the harm of its owners,

Ecclesiastes 5:18, 19

This is what I have observed to be good: that it is appropriate for a person to eat, to drink and to find satisfaction in their toilsome labor under the sun during the few days of life God has given them—for this is their lot. Moreover, when God gives someone wealth and possessions, and the ability to enjoy them, to accept their lot and be happy in their toil—this is a gift of God.

Ecclesiastes 7:11-14

Wisdom, like an inheritance, is a good thing and benefits those who see the sun. Wisdom is a shelter as money is a shelter, but the advantage of knowledge is this: Wisdom preserves those who have it. Consider what God has done: Who can straighten what he has made crooked? When times are good, be happy; but when times are bad, consider this: God has made the one as well as the other. Therefore, no one can discover anything about their future.

Ecclesiastes 9:10, 11

Whatever your hand finds to do, do it with all your might, for in the realm of the dead, where you are going, there is neither working nor planning nor knowledge nor wisdom. I have seen something else under the sun: The race is not to the swift or the battle to the strong, nor does food come to the wise or wealth to the brilliant or favor to the learned; but time and chance happen to them all.

Ecclesiastes 10:18

Through laziness, the rafters sag; because of idle hands, the house leaks.

Ecclesiastes 10:19

A feast is made for laughter, wine makes life merry, and money is the answer for everything.

Ecclesiastes 11:1-6

Ship your grain across the sea; after many days you may receive a return. Invest in seven ventures, yes, in eight; you do not know what disaster may come upon the land. If clouds are full of water, they pour rain on the earth. Whether a tree falls to the south or to the north, in the place where it falls, there it will lie. Whoever watches the wind will not plant; whoever looks at the clouds will not reap. As you do not know the path of the wind, or how the body is formed in a mother's womb, so you cannot understand the work of God, the Maker of all things. Sow your seed in the morning, and at evening let your hands not be idle, for you do not know which will succeed, whether this or that, or whether both will do equally well.

Isaiah 1:19, 20

If you are willing and obedient, you will eat the good things of the land; but if you resist and rebel, you will be devoured by the sword." For the mouth of the LORD has spoken.

Isaiah 32:17-20

The fruit of that righteousness will be peace; its effect will be quietness and confidence forever. My people will live in peaceful dwelling places, in secure homes, in undisturbed places of rest. Though hail flattens the forest and the city is leveled completely, how blessed you will be, sowing your seed by every stream, and letting your cattle and donkeys range free.

Isaiah 51:2, 3

look to Abraham, your father, and to Sarah, who gave you birth. When I called him he was only one man, and I blessed him and made him many. The LORD will surely comfort Zion and will look with compassion on all her ruins; he will make her deserts like Eden, her wastelands like the garden of the LORD. Joy and gladness will be found in her, thanksgiving and the sound of singing.

Jeremiah 4:3

This is what the LORD says to the people of Judah and to Jerusalem: "Break up your unplowed ground and do not sow among thorns.

Jeremiah 17:5-8

This is what the LORD says: "Cursed is the one who trusts in man, who draws strength from mere flesh and whose heart turns away from the LORD. That person will be like a bush in the wastelands; they will not see prosperity when it comes. They will dwell in the parched places of the desert, in a salt land where no one lives. "But blessed is the one who trusts in the LORD, whose confidence is in him. They will be like a tree planted by the water that sends out its roots by the stream. It does not fear when heat comes; its leaves are always green. It has no worries in a year of drought and never fails to bear fruit."

Joel 2:23-27

Be glad, people of Zion, rejoice in the LORD your God, for he has given you the autumn rains because he is faithful. He sends you abundant showers, both autumn and spring rains, as before. The threshing floors will be filled with grain; the vats will overflow with new wine and oil. "I will repay you for the years the locusts have eaten— the great locust and the young locust, the other locusts and the locust swarm— my great army that I sent among you. You will have plenty to eat, until you are full, and you will praise the name of the LORD your God, who has worked wonders for you; never again will my people be shamed. Then you will know that I am in Israel, that I am the LORD your God, and that there is no other; never again will my people be shamed.

Amos 9:13

"The days are coming," declares the LORD, "when the reaper will be overtaken by the plowman and the planter by the one treading grapes. New wine will drip from the mountains and flow from all the hills,

Zechariah 8:12

"The seed will grow well, the vine will yield its fruit, the ground will produce its crops, and the heavens will drop their dew. I will give all these things as an inheritance to the remnant of this people.

New Testament

Matthew 6:19-21

"Do not store up for yourselves treasures on earth, where moths and vermin destroy, and where thieves break in and steal. But store up for yourselves treasures in heaven, where moths and vermin do not destroy, and where thieves do not break in and steal. For where your treasure is, there your heart will be also.

Matthew 13:11, 12

He replied, "Because the knowledge of the secrets of the kingdom of heaven has been given to you, but not to them. Whoever has will be given more, and they will have an abundance. Whoever does not have, even what they have will be taken from them.

Matthew 19:21

Jesus answered, "If you want to be perfect, go, sell your possessions and give to the poor, and you will have treasure in heaven. Then come, follow me."

Mark 4:14-20

The farmer sows the word. Some people are like seed along the path, where the word is sown. As soon as they hear it, Satan comes and takes away the word that was sown in them. Others, like seed sown on rocky places, hear the word and at once receive it with joy. But since they have no root, they last only a short time. When trouble or persecution comes because of the word, they quickly fall away. Still others, like seed sown among thorns, hear the word; but the worries of this life, the deceitfulness of wealth and the desires for other things come in and choke the word, making it unfruitful. Others, like seed sown on good soil, hear the word, accept it, and produce a crop—some thirty, some sixty, some a hundred times what was sown."

Mark 12:41-44

Jesus sat down opposite the place where the offerings were put and watched the crowd putting their money into the temple treasury. Many rich people threw in large amounts. But a poor widow came and put in two very small copper coins, worth only a few cents. Calling his disciples to him, Jesus said, "Truly I tell you, this poor widow has put more into the treasury than all the others. They all gave out of their wealth; but she, out of her poverty, put in everything—all she had to live on."

Luke 12:13-15

Someone in the crowd said to him, "Teacher, tell my brother to divide the inheritance with me." Jesus replied, "Man, who appointed me a judge or an arbiter between you?" Then he said to them, "Watch out! Be on your guard against all kinds of greed; life does not consist in an abundance of possessions."

Luke 12:32-34

"Do not be afraid, little flock, for your Father has been pleased to give you the kingdom. Sell your possessions and give to the poor. Provide purses for yourselves that will not wear out, a treasure in heaven that will never fail, where no thief comes near and no moth destroys. For where your treasure is, there your heart will be also.

Luke 16:9-13

I tell you, use worldly wealth to gain friends for yourselves, so that when it is gone, you will be welcomed into eternal dwellings. "Whoever can be trusted with very little can also be trusted with much, and whoever is dishonest with very little will also be dishonest with much. So if you have not been trustworthy in handling worldly wealth, who will trust you with true riches? And if you have not been trustworthy with someone else's property, who will give you property of your own? "No one can serve two masters. Either you will hate the one and love the other, or you will be devoted to the one and despise the other. You cannot serve both God and money."

John 15:1-8

"I am the true vine, and my Father is the gardener. He cuts off every branch in me that bears no fruit, while every branch that does bear fruit he prunes so that it will be even more fruitful. You are already clean because of the word I have spoken to you. Remain in me, as I also remain in you. No branch can bear fruit by itself; it must remain in the vine. Neither can you bear fruit unless you remain in me. "I am the vine; you are the branches. If you remain in me and I in you, you will bear much fruit; apart from me you can do nothing. If you do not remain in me, you are like a branch that is thrown away and withers; such branches are picked up, thrown into the fire and burned. If you remain in me and my words remain in you, ask whatever you wish, and it will be done for you. This is to my Father's glory, that you bear much fruit, showing yourselves to be my disciples.

1 Corinthians 9:9-11

For it is written in the Law of Moses: "Do not muzzle an ox while it is treading out the grain." Is it about oxen that God is concerned? Surely he says this for us, doesn't he? Yes, this was written for us, because whoever plows and threshes should be able to do so in the hope of sharing in the harvest. If we have sown spiritual seed among you, is it too much if we reap a material harvest from you?

1 Corinthians 13:1-3

If I speak in the tongues of men or of angels, but do not have love, I am only a resounding gong or a clanging cymbal. If I have the gift of prophecy and can fathom all mysteries and all knowledge, and if I have a faith that can move mountains, but do not have love, I am nothing. If I give all I possess to the poor and give over my body to hardship that I may boast, but do not have love, I gain nothing.

2 Corinthians 8:7-9

But since you excel in everything—in faith, in speech, in knowledge, in complete earnestness and in the love we have kindled in you—see that you also excel in this grace of giving. I am not commanding you, but I want to test the sincerity of your love by comparing it with the earnestness of others. For you know the grace of our Lord Jesus Christ, that though he was rich, yet for your sake he became poor, so that you through his poverty might become rich.

2 Corinthians 9:6-15

Remember this: Whoever sows sparingly will also reap sparingly, and whoever sows generously will also reap generously. Each of you should give what you have decided in your heart to give, not reluctantly or under compulsion, for God loves a cheerful giver. And God is able to bless you abundantly, so that in all things at all times, having all that you need, you will abound in every good work. As it is written: "They have freely scattered their gifts to the poor; their righteousness endures forever." Now he who supplies seed to the sower and bread for food will also supply and increase your store of seed and will enlarge the harvest of your righteousness. You will be enriched in every way so that you can be generous on every occasion, and through us your generosity will result in thanksgiving to God. This service that you perform is not only supplying the needs of the Lord's people but is also overflowing in many expressions of thanks to God. Because of the service by which you have proved yourselves, others will praise God for the obedience that accompanies your confession of the gospel of Christ, and for your generosity in sharing with them and with everyone else. And in their prayers for you their hearts will go out to you, because of the surpassing grace God has given you. Thanks be to God for his indescribable gift!

Galatians 6:4-10

Each one should test their own actions. Then they can take pride in themselves alone, without comparing themselves to someone else, for each one should carry their own load. Nevertheless, the one who receives instruction in the word should share all good things with their instructor. Do not be deceived: God cannot be mocked. A man reaps what he sows. Whoever sows to please their flesh, from the flesh will reap destruction; whoever sows to please the Spirit, from the Spirit will reap eternal life. Let us not become weary in doing good, for at the proper time we will reap a harvest if we do not give up. Therefore, as we have opportunity, let us do good to all people, especially to those who belong to the family of believers.

1 Thessalonians 4:10-11

And in fact, you do love all of God's family throughout Macedonia. Yet we urge you, brothers and sisters, to do so more and more, and to make it your ambition to lead a quiet life: You should mind your own business and work with your hands, just as we told you,

1 Timothy 6:6-10

But godliness with contentment is great gain. For we brought nothing into the world, and we can take nothing out of it. But if we have food and clothing, we will be content with that. Those who want to get rich fall into temptation and a trap and into many foolish and harmful desires that plunge people into ruin and destruction. For the love of money is a root of all kinds of evil. Some people, eager for money, have wandered from the faith and pierced themselves with many griefs.

1 Timothy 6:17-19

Command those who are rich in this present world not to be arrogant nor to put their hope in wealth, which is so uncertain, but to put their hope in God, who richly provides us with everything for our enjoyment. Command them to do good, to be rich in good deeds, and to be generous and willing to share. In this way they will lay up treasure for themselves as a firm foundation for the coming age, so that they may take hold of the life that is truly life.

Hebrews 6:10-15

God is not unjust; he will not forget your work and the love you have shown him as you have helped his people and continue to help them. We want each of you to show this same diligence to the very end, so that what you hope for may be fully realized. We do not want you to become lazy, but to imitate those who through faith and patience inherit what has been promised. When God made his promise to Abraham, since there was no one greater for him to swear by, he swore by himself, saying, "I will surely bless you and give you many descendants." And so after waiting patiently, Abraham received what was promised.

Hebrews 10:34-36

You suffered along with those in prison and joyfully accepted the confiscation of your property, because you knew that you yourselves had better and lasting possessions. So do not throw away your confidence; it will be richly rewarded. You need to persevere so that when you have done the will of God, you will receive what he has promised.

James 1:2-4

Consider it pure joy, my brothers and sisters, whenever you face trials of many kinds, because you know that the testing of your faith produces perseverance. Let perseverance finish its work so that you may be mature and complete, not lacking anything.

James 2:5

Listen, my dear brothers and sisters: Has not God chosen those who are poor in the eyes of the world to be rich in faith and to inherit the kingdom he promised those who love him?

James 2:14-18

What good is it, my brothers and sisters, if someone claims to have faith but has no deeds? Can such faith save them? Suppose a brother or a sister is without clothes and daily food. If one of you says to them, "Go in peace; keep warm and well fed," but does nothing about their physical needs, what good is it? In the same way, faith by itself, if it is not accompanied by action, is dead. But someone will say, "You have faith; I have deeds." Show me your faith without deeds, and I will show you my faith by my deeds.

ENDNOTES

1. According to the *World Vision Canada* article "Hard Facts On Poverty." See http://www.worldvision.ca/GetInvolved/ Youth-Action-Zone/Pages/hard-facts-on-poverty.aspx and http://www.worldvision.ca/Education-and-Justice/ advocacy-in-action/Pages/the-hard-facts.aspx.
2. Dakes Annotated Reference Bible
3. "sow." *Merriam-Webster Online Dictionary*. 2011. http://www.merriam-webster.com (15 March 2011).

MORE RESOURCES
FROM JOSHUA & JANET ANGELA MILLS

For additional copies of this book, more information about live spiritual training seminars, The Intensified Glory Institute®, and other glory resources, please contact the ministry of Joshua & Janet Angela Mills.

NEW WINE INTERNATIONAL

In USA: PO Box 4037, Palm Springs, CA 92263

In Canada: 47-20821 Fraser Hwy, Suite #450, Langley BC V3A 0B6

Toll-free 1-866-60-NEW-WINE

Online 24/7 www.NewWineInternational.org

BULK ORDER DISCOUNTS FOR MINISTRIES, CHURCHES & CHRISTIAN RETAILERS:

Discounts are available to all churches, ministries and bookstores that desire to place large quantity orders. For more information please email: product@newwineinternational.org.

Dear Friend,

I believe that you are a kingdom connection! God wants to use you to make a difference in the lives of thousands around the world. Do you believe that?

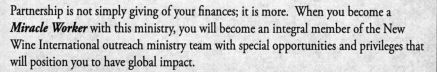

I would like to invite you to become a *Miracle Worker* with me, and help me take this supernatural message of Jesus Christ and His glory to the far corners of the earth.

Partnership is not simply giving of your finances; it is more. When you become a *Miracle Worker* with this ministry, you will become an integral member of the New Wine International outreach ministry team with special opportunities and privileges that will position you to have global impact.

A *"Miracle Worker"* is a person who agrees to:
1. Financially support the ministry of New Wine International (NWI)
2. Pray faithfully for Joshua & Janet Angela Mills and the NWI Ministry Team as they carry the message of Jesus Christ around the world.
3. Pray for those who will receive ministry through NWI ministry events and resources.

Partnership is not only what you can do to help me, but also what I can do to help you. Becoming a *Miracle Worker* with NWI provides a covenant agreement between you and me. By being a *Miracle Worker,* you will connect with the anointing and glory on this ministry as I send you monthly updates and revelatory teachings on the glory realm. You will receive my continued prayer for you and your family and you will be linked with the unique anointing that is on this ministry for unusual signs and wonders.

There are currently several ways to partner with NWI. I want you to decide the partnership level according to what the Lord has placed in your heart to do.

In His Great Love,

Joshua Mills

P.S. *Call my office today to become a partner or register online so that I can send you a special **Miracle Worker** Welcome Package filled with special benefits and information.*

Toll-Free: **1-866-60-NEW-WINE**
Online 24/7:
www.NewWineInternational.org
www.PartnersInPraise.com

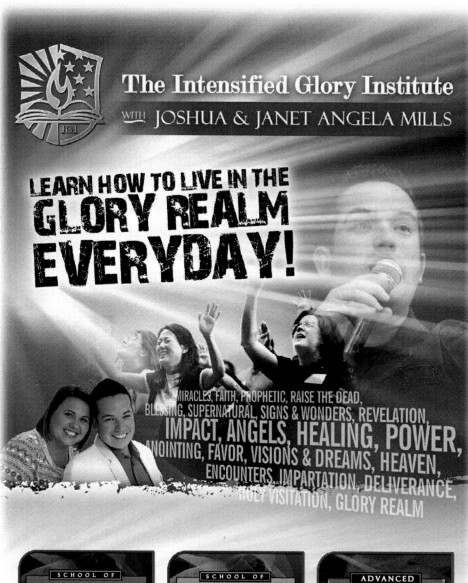

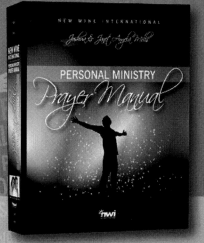